WISE LIKE SNAKES,
INNOCENT LIKE DOVES

Thirty Biblical Reflections in Feminist Perspective

ii

WISE LIKE SNAKES, INNOCENT LIKE DOVES

Thirty Biblical Reflections in Feminist Perspective

Gabriele Dietrich

ISPCK
Impacting Communities since 1710

TTS

2011

Wise like Snakes, Innocent like Doves – Published by the Rev. Dr. Ashish Amos of Indian Society for Promoting Christian Knowledge (ISPCK), Post Box 1585, 1654 Madarsa Road, Kashmere Gate, Delhi- 110006 for Tamil Theological Seminary, Arasaradi, Madurai - 625 016 under the Women's Empowerment Program (WEP-26).

© Author, 2011

ISBN: 978-81-8465-146-1

Laser typeset by **ISPCK,** Post Box 1585,
1654 Madarsa Road, Kashmere Gate, Delhi-110006
Tel: 23866322, 23866323
e-mail–ashish@ispck.org.in • ella@ispck.org.in
website-www.ispck.org.

Dedicated to
my maternal grandmother
Hedwig Kolander Schwarzrock
who would have become a pastor, had she been a boy.
Instead, she brought up three kids as a refugee and
war widow by tailoring and later abandoned faith
because God had "allowed" two world wars to
happen in her life time.

CONTENTS

FOREWORD

I consider it a great privilege to have been asked to write a foreword to this collection of Bible studies and sermons delivered on different occasions by Gabriele. Although they were delivered on different occasions, the common perspective that knits them together is the feminist perspective.

We have imbibed patriarchal language and sentiment. Therefore, even when God speaks with the fondness of a mother, we only think and speak of God in masculine conceptions. The studies of Gabriele make a good attempt to reverse this ingrained tendency. As a Bible teacher I realize that I never used to bother to make the special effort needed to make a large majority of male students understand this. I did however, point to passages which explicitly refer to God as mother bird, as mother who brought liberation by breast feeding the children of Israel yoked under slavery and leads them gently towards freedom. There are only a few passages in the Bible which speak of God as mother explicitly.

The other lesson that gets effectively communicated is that women are the source and sustenance of life. The day when this will be openly acknowledged is an end time hope which will come after the experience of tribulation.

This latter lesson is brought to us through bringing in contemporary experience of many struggles, some of them in and around Madurai and yet others from the story of the Adivasi people forcefully uprooted for building the Sardar Sarovar Dam in Gujarat and the valiant struggle against that even by courageously facing the on coming waters. This experience challenges all those of us believers in the resurrection in a doctrinal and theoretical way. And most of those who stood in the waters willing to face death without any hope in the resurrection were women, Gabriele reminds us.

As a New Testament teacher I was very much intrigued by the way Gabriele treats Luke's narrative of the Resurrection of Jesus, neatly belittling the witness of women and totally refusing to give even a second place to the fact the risen Jesus appearing to Mary Magdalene. I have always tried to excuse Luke on the grounds that he gives pride of place to Mary the Mother of Jesus. Luke indirectly alludes to what Mary had kept in her heart as the source of his story. And therefore explain the reference to the disciples dismissing the testimony of the women as an idle tale, as a deliberate attempt to show the male disciples in a bad light, with regard to their attitude about women. However, Gabriele's careful study of the text tradition which refers to Peter visiting the tomb but returning wondering only about the folded linen and then without a narrative that Jesus had appeared to Peter, does show that perhaps he wanted to give a place of honor to Peter the Galilean in spite of his preference for Jerusalem. But then Gabriele also points out the stern rebuke of Jesus of the disciples on their way to Emmaus. So perhaps the confusion is due to a definite clash of perspective.

Gabriele is a careful scholar and an incisive social analyst. But she certainly is not an arm chair scholar; she is a full time activist. Where does she find the time to combine all these commitments? The illustrations she narrates are from her actions of solidarity in the local situation as well as, as a National Coordinator of the National Alliance of the People's Movements. Where does Gabriele find the time, much more, the perspective to have a vision against adversity? The way she integrates learning and experience to bring about a new awareness is most impressive. Gabriele would have us all become aware that we are involved in a slow process full of set backs and disappointments. But that should not deter us, for there is hope. This message is most needed, may no one give up due to frustrations and disappointments.

I do hope the English version will bring clarity to the far too many mistranslations and hard to understand Tamil expressions in the Tamil first edition.

I commend this collection, well arranged under different relevant themes, wholeheartedly.

                                        Dhyanchand Carr

PREFACE

This collection of sermons and Bible studies originated from my work on the faculty of Tamil Nadu Theological Seminary (TTS) in Madurai. Nearly all of these reflections were presented by me in Tamil in the chapel of TTS in the context of a Sunday service or a Bible study in the early morning. These texts were first published in Tamil in 2007, but there were many requests to make them accessible in English as well. This proved to be difficult, because some texts did not exist in English or the English version had been lost. I am deeply thankful to Mr. Gnana Surabimani for helping me to put some of these texts into English after the Tamil had been brushed up by experts, so that sometimes I could not recognise my own thoughts any longer. Mr. Surabimani also helped to bundle these reflections under certain headings. The order is topical, not chronological. This has also to do with the fact that not all texts could be identified by dates.

The difficulty in a place like TTS is the fact that it is a changing community of theological students and teachers and their families, while at the same time destitute and sexually exploited women also attend and large numbers of children are milling around. Some of the reflections were presented in the form of skits and dialogues, interspersed with song and dance.

Often the services were worked out collectively with elaborate liturgies. We also frequently used the village liturgies of our colleague Parattai (Theophilus Appavoo). Looking back at it all I realise that this English rendering only gives a rather pale picture of something much more colourful. However, I felt it was worth making this effort, because I have also done work in the North Eastern states (mostly Nagaland and Mizoram) as well as Myanmar and have held Bible studies there, which are not part of this volume. In those parts, biblical interpretation tends to be much more fundamentalist, but to the extent that people get acquainted with social analysis, they also want to get into biblical reflections of a different nature. So I do hope that sharing from the experiences in TTS will help theological rethinking in others parts as well.

It will be clear from these texts that they are very much in dialogue with secular society and with people's movements in different parts of the country. In my understanding this is a great challenge to the churches to transcend their boundaries and learn from experiences of struggle and transformation. The title of this book is taken from Matt. 10,16 where the disciples are sent out as sheep in the midst of wolves. Being wise as serpents and innocent as doves has a strong connection to the wisdom tradition, which comes through in several places in this collection.

I am thankful to my colleague Rev. Adlin Reginabai and to Mr. Manikandan and John Wilson, who collected many of these texts on stencils in the olden days. I also thank Ms.Pappa for typing it all on the computer and going through many corrections. Last but not least, I thank Bas Wielenga, who has been patient with my unorthodox interpretations and who kept our house well stocked with biblical commentaries. I also thank my children Karuna and Prasad, who frequently helped me to get through the stress of these Tamil services, by being effortlessly bi-lingual and very supportive. I thank the changing community of

TTS for giving room to a great variety of people without losing its culture.

Gabriele Dietrich

I. Love

2

1. LOVE IN DIVISIVENESS
(Leviticus 19:9-18 and 1 Corinthians 13)

The texts for this Sunday are dealing with situations of fragmentation and divisiveness. While Israel was in exile, it was necessary to gather strength again. They had to redistribute scarce resources, to strengthen the weak. God gives his directions of social justice, saying at every juncture: I am the Lord which literally means: I shall be with you. It is because of the promise of God`s presence that the people are encouraged to love one another. The contents of this love are spelled out in terms of social justice: it is necessary to provide for the poor and the sojourner. Don`t steal, don`t cheat, don`t lie, don`t withhold wages, be helpful to the handicapped, don`t slander, be not resentful or judgemental and grudging. Argue your case tenaciously and patiently. Love your neighbour as yourself. It is obvious that all the weaknesses of any close-knit community are attacked here. Yet the promise of God is: I shall be with you and therefore you shall love one another.

This tradition of love rooted in social justice goes back to the most crucial commandment of the people of Israel: Schma Israel, listen Israel, the Lord your God is one and you shall love the Lord your God with your heart undivided. There is no place for double standards here, one set of values for religious use and one for day to day "adjustments". In the tradition of Israel, faith has to be lived.

It is this Jewish tradition of love of which Paul reminds the people in Corinth in their crisis. The people of Corinth have a lot of difference between rich and poor in their parish. It is the rich businessmen, the traders, the scribes, the educated who quote the Hebrew scripture, and try to control the contents of theology. But it is the poor workers from the harbour, the loadmen, the casual workers, the uneducated who protest by speaking in tongues. The Spirit cannot find other expression in them. They come under the leadership of the red Chloe, a very outspoken woman, from the harbour of Corinth and create disorder. The literates are quoting Paul and claim the spirit of prophecy. The illiterates under the leadership of a woman claim the Holy Spirit. They want to have their say, but find it difficult to make themselves understood.

It is in this situation of division, fragmentation and disorder, where the outcastes are trying to assert themselves in their own cultural terms that Paul has to take a stand.

Paul reminds the people of the tradition of Israel. God`s presence enables people to love one another. The speaking in tongues has no meaning unless there is love. But the prophecy too has no meaning unless there is love. Even if I have enough faith to remove mountains and deliver my body to be burnt, there is no meaning if I lack love.

It we look into the verses 4-7 of 1 Cor.13, we find a love described which we normally ascribe to mothers: Patient, kind, selfless and humble, not irritable and resentful. Love bears all things, believes all things, hopes all things endures all things. It is the kind of love for which we glorify motherhood. I finally want to put these verses into our own context and ask what they mean for us today. Of course we can conveniently use them against the evangelical and Pentecostals who edify themselves individually and we can make a claim that ours is the spirit of prophecy. We can congratulate ourselves for our consciousness about the poor, the dalits, the women, the ecology and consider the churches as backward.

However, things are not as simple as that. We need to remind ourselves of the deep crisis of the economy and of our political life which our community and our state are going through. The political and social fabric have deteriorated very badly. We are in a situation in which it is very hard to intervene meaningfully. Our own prophetic stereotypes about liberation may sound to many people as it we were speaking in tongues: unintelligible. Striving for love, patience, to listen and reach deeper clarity, will be our challenge in this situation. Let us be humble enough to meet this challenge and let us assure each other of God's love which will be present among us.

- Amen.

(September 25, 1988)

* * * *

2. THE PRODIGAL SON

Luke 15:11-12
(Interpretation in the form of a skit)

1. Read Lk.15:1-12

Scene 1: Younger son comes and asks for his share of property. Wants to go out, see the world, have experiences, work, study.

The father reflects:

What is this? Does this boy want to bury me alive? Can we divide the land on which our family lives? Will we not perish in times of need?

But who am I to deny him his own life? Is it for me to hold on to property? And do I not have the oldest son? Will he not be with me and look after me? Do I value my own security more than my child's dreams? But what will happen to him? Will he not perish? Must I not protect him and teach him to look after his security? Will he not hurt himself?

2. Read Lk.15:13-16

Scene 2: The son goes round drinking and womanising. He falls down drunk. He cries: I am hungry! There is no food anywhere. Everything has vanished. There is only famine! Is there no one to feed me. *Appa, Amma! Pasikuthu.*

3. Read Lk.15:17-24

Scene 3: Son speaks to himself: I must come to myself. I have been out of my mind. Is this me? *Amma, Appa,* take me at least as your servant. I am not worthy to be your servant. I am not worthy to be your son. I have let everything go to the dogs.

Father is looking out from afar. So long since my son is gone. I hear there has been famine all over. Will he still be alive? Have I lost my son? Should I not have held him back? What is that? Someone coming? Is it him? He runs: *Maganaa Neeya?* Have you come? Embraces and kisses him.

Son: *Appa! Naan Thappu Seithein!* I have sinned against you and sinned against heaven. I am not worthy to be your son.

Father calls everyone: Come, come, everyone, bring him sandals for his feet and a ring for his finger, bring him food to eat and come let`s all sing and dance. My son was dead and is alive. He was lost and is found. Let us celebrate!

4. Read V.25-32

Scene 4: Two women at the water tap talking:

First woman: Mariamma, did you hear? Our neighbour`s youngest son has come home? Do you hear the music? They are celebrating. Good for nothing this young fellow. Just runs away and drinks and whores around. And the old man just runs and embraces him and throws a party. Will it not encourage other young good for nothings?

Second woman: Karuthammal how can you talk like this? Has the old man not cried everyday of his life that this son may live and come to himself? Has he not been generous in his love and honoured his son's life more than the property?

First woman: But what about the first boy? He was hard working and obedient; and has been slogging all these years! Do you think the old man has ever as much as noticed him? Does he have to make such a fuss about the young chap? What will his *Annan* feel. He feels so taken for granted!

Second woman: But the old man has shared everything with his oldest son, he has kept nothing for himself !

Annan standing on the side, fuming. Appa, Amma have you forgotten me? Where am I in your eyes, in your heart?

Servant comes and calls: Your brother has come, Your father has killed the fatted calf, because he has received him safe and sound.

Son says: Get lost!

Father comes out and pleads. Son says: Leave me, I can`t come! Have you ever bothered about me? I have obeyed you all along. Have I ever had as much as a kid to throw a party with my friends? And this good for nothing fellow who has squandered all your livelihood, you kill a calf for him.

Father: My son, you are always with me. All that is mine is yours. Your brother who was lost has been found. He was dead and he is alive! Come and join the dance!

Sing: Lord of the Dance.

Reflection:

Who is this God who speaks to us in this parable? Is he the all loving, accepting God of infinite generosity who does not want to keep anything for himself and allows his children to walk in freedom even if they hurt themselves?

Or is he a God who takes obedience for granted and does not even notice and acknowledge it when it is given? Is he the generous father who comes running when his son returns or is he the insensitive father who cares only for the lost ones and not for those who stay loyal? Is it enough when he says to the faithful son: You are always with me, mine is yours? Could he not have done more than that?

Is it enough when he finally goes and calls the eldest son? He has changed in his patriarchal demands towards his youngest son. But has he truly turned his heart towards his eldest son? Has he changed toward him?

And we, where are we? Are we the young son who needs to run away in order to finally come to himself? Or are we the elder brother who judges his *thambi* (brother) and judges his father for being so overjoyed at his return. Are we pleading with God for acceptance? Can we be whole in ourselves and join the dance? Can we join the dance for the sake of peace and the larger community? Do we join the dance coming to ourselves in our hearts` gladness?

(October 5, 1999)

* * * *

3. BUS STOP LESSONS

Luke 9:23-27

Last year, I met one of my Hindu neighbours at a bus stop. In the middle of the crowd he came and asked me a question. It was obviously very important to him: Do you Christians really believe that we Hindus cannot achieve salvation?, he asked. There are many different views on this, I said. But I believe you should read what Jesus himself told his disciples as it is written in Matt.25. The crucial question there is what have people done in their life. Those who have done God's will, may not even be aware of it. They may have been pious people, but they did not notice what needed to be done.

My neighbour was quite happy when he heard this. "Yes, we have to serve others that is most important" he said. "Shall I tell you what to me is the essence of the Bible?" he asked. "If any man would come after me, let him deny himself and take up his cross daily and follow me". We have to do God`s will even if it pains. It is like a doctor cutting a boil. It has to be cut so that it can heal. But it will pain. So we have to go ahead and do our duty even if it pains greatly.

I felt quite encouraged by my neighbours words because I was at a point in my life where I found it very difficult to forge ahead and do my duty. All the same, I remained puzzled: first of all, how does one know what one`s duty is? Secondly, how does one bear the pain?

In order to answer these questions, my neighbour was referring to the 12th chapter of the Bhagvad Gita, v.13: "He who hates no creature and is friendly and compassionate towards all, who is free from the feeling 'I and mine', even-minded in pain and pleasure, forbearing, ever content, steady in meditation, self-controlled and possessed of firm conviction, with mind and intellect fixed on Me-, he who is devoted to Me is dear to Me". Thus says Krishna.

So his answer was: *nishkama karma,* non-attached action, action without asking for the fruits. You concentrate on God and do your duty and gain peace of mind. I tried to relate this answer to the life of Christ. Of course, Jesus also did not ask for the fruits of deeds because he was not after success. But he was also not after peace of mind. He could become very angry and at many occasions he shed tears of compassion and of anger. He was attached to the world because he loved it. Jesus` love for people defines, what is duty. Duty is born out of love for others and it can be in total contrast and conflict with the dharma with which one is born. But love will also help to bear the pain when we violate the existing order.

Incidentally, I met another friend a little later. He is neither a Hindu nor a Christian, he is a Marxist. He never had a Christian up-bringing. But he sometimes quotes the Bible to me. What he has to say, makes me read the Bible in a different light. It also makes me read the Bhagavad Gita in a different light. He often refers to the same text as my Hindu neighbour. He does not talk of the Cross. But he often says: "What does it profit a man if he gains the whole world and loses and forfeits himself". In fact, this could be written as a motto over his whole life. He has given up a secure position and a good salary. He became a full-timer in political work. His family has often grumbled because of this.

It means so much insecurity in financial matters and often even persecution and harassment. His lifestyle really goes against the dharma of a householder. But he does his work not asking for the fruits. The fruits cannot be seen either today or tomorrow. The revolution will take a long time. He also is free from feeling of "I and mine". He is not after his personal advantage. He even tries to abolish the private ownership of means of production. Certainly, private profit from other people's work is the summit of saying "I and mine". But this does not mean that he is impartial or non-attached. Like Jesus, he can become very angry and I have seen tears of compassion in his eyes. He is not after his own peace of mind and he disturbs other people's peace of mind.

If I look back, I notice that my Hindu friend has taught me something about the cross. On the other hand, my Marxist friend has taught me something about the Kingdom of God. Both together have helped me understand the ninth chapter of Luke's Gospel much better.

To follow Christ means to follow the road towards the Kingdom of God, and this road leads to suffering. In the beginning of the chapter Jesus sends his disciples out. They should only keep the bare necessities and share with everyone. In the same chapter, we hear also how Jesus shares the five loaves and two fishes with the crowds. Everyone is encouraged to share what they have. In the end they are all fed and there still is surplus. The economy of sharing is a sign of God's Kingdom. But this does not mean at all that there is security on the road to God`s Kingdom. The road leads through suffering. This is summarized at the end of the chapter: "The foxes have holes and the birds have nests but the Son of Man has no where to lay his head". The road to the Kingdom of God does not lead us to peace of mind. The road to the Kingdom breaks us away from the existing order of inequality, of profit and exploitation, of "I and mine". But if we look towards the Kingdom of God, the new order of love and equality, we will also know our duty. It will be painful to go on this road. It may bring us into conflict with what we formerly considered to be our duty. We may meet our Hindu friend there on the road, we may meet our Marxist friend there on the road. We may perhaps miss one of our Christian friends there. If on the way we learn to love one another and to share with each other, we may learn how to bear the pain.

(1980)

* * * *

4. NOTHING IS UNTOUCHABLE IN GOD'S CREATION

Matthew 8: 1-17

We will take a look at three incidents mentioned in the Gospel of Matthew and how Jesus healed the sick. In all the three, Jesus healed the marginalized people.

Let us first take the healing of a leper. People considered lepers to be untouchables. Due to his guts and his faith in the acts of Jesus, this leper pleaded with Jesus to make him clean. Jesus touched the man and healed him. Unlike in the healing incidents that take place nowadays, Jesus instructed the leper not to tell anyone about it. However, he told him, "....go, show yourself to the priest and offer the gift Moses commanded, as a testimony." This incident shows us how Jesus enabled a sick person, marginalized by the society as an untouchable, to be accepted by it. He also creates an evidence for his action.

The next incident concerns the servant of a centurion. He is a man beset with two different problems. That he is a servant is one problem. That he is the servant, specifically, of a centurion serving in the army, is yet another problem. Since people have experienced suffering, cruelties and loss of precious lives because of the army, the centurion must have incurred their wrath. When an army man does not enjoy the support of the people, how can he seek help from people under his custody? Nevertheless, Jesus was getting ready to go to the house of the hated centurion. The centurion knew that his power would be futile before the ideas, thoughts and acts of Jesus. He was aware that his power would not be acceptable to Jesus. But, since Jesus had the power to heal diseases, he wanted Jesus to exercise his power. He wanted to save Jesus the embarrassment to come to the house of a centurion. He expressed his trust that Jesus can command the illness of the servant to leave him. The power Jesus had was not due to carrying weapons. It was different. Even though Jesus had known about the centurion, he was prepared to go to his house. For, unlike others, the centurion was asking Jesus for his servant to be cured, not for himself. But Jesus realizes the faith of the centurion in his non-violent power. He says:" Go, be it done for you as you have believed."

The third incident relates to the mother-in-law of Peter. We do not know what she asked Jesus and what Jesus replied. However, we come to know from the Bible that when Jesus touched her hand, fever left her and she got up and began to wait on him. After that, he went on to cure many who were possessed and sick.

All the three incidents tell us a few significant points about the healing of people. The first incident reveals that there is no such thing as untouchability in the creation of God. We should become one with the people and touch them. Healing requires touching. The second incident shows that the ministry of Jesus was not only to heal the sick and touch the marginalized but also to show love even towards enemies. The third incident brings out the fact that Jesus sets right the unequal relationships among people. He touched and healed a woman, who was part of the life world of his disciples, but about whom we do not hear otherwise. We also hear that Jesus could set right all kinds of madness in the society around him.

Can we try to follow Jesus in his footsteps by learning from his approach?

Note: All the three incidents were first enacted as skits.

* * * *

5. SPIRITUALITY OF ADMINISTRATION
Colossians 3:9-17

In today's spirituality workshop we are reflecting on the problem of church administration. This is an important topic, because once we go to the churches, we are in the clutches of administration. While we are in the seminary, we are into theology, studies, exposures, spirituality. Once we are in the church, we are into institutions, into rivalries, quarrels, competitions, court cases. How do we relate this to our faith? Is there a spirituality of administration? This is the question on which we have to reflect today. For this, I have chosen this text of Col.3:9-17. Of course, the ancient church in Colossae was not the kind of institution which we have today. Today, the quarrels are often simply over money, land, outright power struggles. The conflicts in those days may have been different. But the point is: the conflicts distort the image of Christ. We cannot see Christ, if we are involved in quarrels. However, obviously, the conflicts are with us and we cannot avoid them. So the question arises: How do we deal with them? How do we approach them?

I would like to say something about the background of the letter. There is a controversy whether it was written by Paul and whether it was written from the jail in Rome. We also do not exactly know what were the conflicts which Paul was dealing with in this congregation. We know that there were different jathis, inams (castes and races). There were Jews and some of them followed a Gnostic religion which required suppression of the body and severe rituals. There may also have been all sorts of other religious observances among non-Jews.

However, the important point lies in Paul`s counter argument. He starts off in our passage by saying some very simple things.

1. We should not lie to one another. We should be truthful.

2. He speaks of the old nature and the new nature, renewed in knowledge after the image of the creator.

3. This relates to a key passage of the whole letter which is a Christ hymn in Col.1:15-20.

This means: Christ is the image of the invisible God.

He is the first form of all creation He was before all things and in him all things are held together: thrones, dominions, principalities, authorities (v.16) - all are created by him and all are held together by him. This means: The new nature is in the image of Christ and in him all things are held together.

So there is no caste, no ethnicity, circumcised, uncircumcised, barbarian, Scythian, slave, free man. Christ is all in all.

This does not mean that differences do not exist. They are there, they are real. It is not like the BJP which says: We do not believe in caste, all this is irrelevant, and then imposes a Brahmin ideology. It just says: these differences cannot be, they have to be overcome.

So this raises the question: How can this be done? We all know that the differences are not just between Brahmins and Dalits, they are between Dalits and OBC's they are among Dalits so much so that finally in UP the Dalit Chief Minister, a Dalit woman, goes with the BJP who is casteist and patriarchal.

Likewise, in the church, much of the time our differences are between Pallar, Parayar, Chakiliar, Dalit and OBC. So how do we over come it?

There is one important point missing here. The text does not say anything about the relationship between male and female. We are not told what happens to men and women. In Gal.3:28 Jews and Greek master and slave, male and female are clearly connected. But in this text in Colossians, women are not made visible. And further down in the household code of this chapter, v.18-25, women are exhorted to be subject to their husbands.

This is not a question which we can deal with here right now as it is a problem which has been made invisible in this text on which we are reflecting. But it is important to remember that in the letters of Paul, there are many contradictions as far as statements on women are concerned. And we should not lose sight of this problem because our way of preserving caste has deeply to do with how we run our families, how we arrange marriages, how we treat women. This we study in depth in the Social Analysis courses and we take it up in peoples movements and in the church so we need both, - knowledge about the image of the creator in whom all are one. We also need to study and know how such unity is destroyed, how the divisions can be overcome.

Verses 12-17 are told about the alternatives, these are given in five steps.

1. The first step is given v.12 and 13. The key words are: compassion, kindness, lowliness, meekness and patience, forbearance.

These are all terms which are in a way suspect. We are often thinking that these qualities have to do with servility, the spirit of slavery. We are making efforts to incite people to struggle. But this is exactly where our problems also arise. In our effort to struggle, we also put ourselves over others, we are judgmental, we vie for power, we breed corruption, and we start telling lies. We forget that Jesus has come as the Suffering Servant, not as the conquering King as M.M.Thomas has pointed out. We normally preach meekness to those who are weak, but here these qualities of compassion, patience and forbearing are preached to those who are in the power struggle, those who are reaching out for power we are encouraged to bring forward our complaints and to forgive one another.

2. The next step is love which binds everything together in perfect harmony. The point is first we have to complain and then forgive. Without this, love is not possible.

3. The next step is peace. Peace not only in our hearts but peace in Christ with whom we are called in one body. So once again, peace of mind is not possible without unity of the body. Peace of mind is not possible if we are divided by caste or as men and women or if some eat and others go hungry. Peace of mind requires material unity.

Let the word of Christ dwell in you richly, teach and admonish one another in all wisdom, and sing psalms and

hymns and spiritual songs with thankfulness in your hearts
to God. (Read v.16)

4. We are finally told how to gain freedom to live all
this. So we need the word of Christ to dwell in us. This
means not only to have the words in our mouth but to live
the word with our bodies and with our social life. For this
we need wisdom to discern and we must turn to each
other in wisdom. We are also encouraged to sing hymns
and spiritual songs with thankfulness in our hearts.

5. And this is the summary of our text - v.17. Whatever
we do in word and deed we do in the name of Jesus
giving thanks to God the Father through him.

I think that this, too, is a criterion for church
administration. Are we using the name of Christ in vain?
Are we acting in his name? And are we able to thank God
for what is happening in the process? Let us thank God
for keeping there questions alive in our mind, Amen.

* * * *

6. A STILL SMALL VOICE

(Biblical Reflection at the Senate of Serampore, Kottayam)

I Kings 19:1-18

The story of Elijah's experience on Mount Horeb is difficult to address. The preceding competition between the Baal's priests and the prophet of JHWH is embarrassing, as it consists of a showdown of miracles and ends in the slaughter of the Baal priests. Of course we can say that it is the battle of a prophet against the imposition of a state religion by a king who married a woman of Sidon (I King 16, 31ff) who imposed her religion on the people violently, possibly involving child sacrifice (v.34). Even this does not take away the smell of blood which chapter 18 leaves behind.

Jezebel sends a messenger who spells revenge on the prophet, threatening him with the same fate like the slain priests. Elijah wanders to the South, reaches Beer-sheba and withdraws into the wilderness. Far from boasting over his spectacular victory, Elijah wants his life to be ended. He is desperate. He says to God: "It is enough, now, O Lord, take away my life, for I am no better than my fathers". He lies down under a broom tree and falls asleep. The bloodstained victory has broken his spirit. It is here that an angel of the Lord touches him and asks him: "Arise and eat". He finds a cake baked on hot stones and a jar of water and eats and drinks and promptly falls asleep again.

But the angel wakes him up again and makes him eat and drink again and on the strength of this food he walks through the desert for forty days and nights till he reaches Mount Horeb in the Sinai Peninsula. The forty days remind of the forty years of the people of Israel in the desert and the forty days of Jesus' fast before the temptation. There he stays in a cave (v9) and the word of the Lord comes to him asking him: "What are you doing here Elijah?" Elijah answers: "I have been jealous for Adonai Zebaoth for the people of Israel have forsaken thy covenant, thrown down the altars and slain the prophets with the sword. And I, even I only, am left, and they seek my life, to take it away". And he is made to stand on Mount Horeb before JHWH.

> "And he said, 'go forth and stand upon the mountain before the Lord.` And behold, the Lord passed by, and a great and strong wind rent the mountains, and broke in pieces the rocks before the Lord, but the Lord was not in the wind, and after the earthquake a fire, but the Lord was not in the fire, and after the fire a still small voice. And when Elijah heard it, he wrapped his face in his mantle and went out and stood at the entrance of the cave. And behold, there came a voice to him, and said,` What are you doing here Elijah?` "

We encounter the furies of nature here, the storm which breaks rocks into pieces and rents the mountains. But God is not in the wind. And after the wind an earthquake, but God is not in the earthquake and after the earthquake, a fire, but God is not in the fire. This is significant, because in the Elijah stories the forces of nature seem to appear as signs of God. The contest with the Baals priests was about forcing fire upon the sacrifice. But God is not in the fire. God is not in the earthquake either.

There have been many voices these days who have
wanted to interpret the earthquake in Gujarat as a
punishment for what had happened to Christians in the
Dangs. But God is not in the earthquake. The only thing
which remains after the wind, the quake and the fire is the
still, small voice. When Elijah hears this, he wraps his face
into his mantle and stands at the entrance of the cave. It
is the stillness of the small voice which speaks.

Then the voice inquires again: "What are you doing
here, Elijah" and Elijah gives the same answer. The voice
sends him to the wilderness of Damascus. He is told to
anoint Hazael as king of Syria and Jehu as King over Israel
and Elisha as the prophet. More bloodshed will be the
result, but there will be 7000 left in Israel who have not
bowed their knees to Baal and have not kissed him. In a
way, Hazael, Jehu and Elisha go parallel to the wind, the
earthquake and the fire. The 7000 who do not bow before
Baal, they go parallel to the still, small voice. Who are they
and what does it mean not to bow before Baal?

Bowing before Baal is idolatry. But what is idolatry?
What is this making of images which rule the mind and
muffle the still small voice? This is not just a contest
between the God of Israel and the gods of Canaan. It is
not about fighting other people's religion and culture. It
is the memory of sovereignty, the liberation from slavery,
vs. autocratic rule of a king who has Naboth killed in a
false case in order to acquire his vineyard. It is not just
the prophet of JHWH against Jezebel, the Sidonite wife of
the Israelite king. It is Elijah who has fed the widow of
Zarephat in Sidon with oil and meal and has revived her
son (Ch.17) vs. the queen from Sidon who cooks up the
case against Nabot to grab the vineyard for her husband.

Jesus quotes the case of this widow of Zarephat when he explains the contents of the Nazareth manifesto in order to illustrate that no prophet is accepted in his own country. He has to go to the aliens to be heard. But he goes to a poor widow, not to the rulers. It is not as if the final defeat of Ahab and Jezebel, the prophecy that they shall be eaten by dogs and birds (Ch.21:20-26), brings any perspective of real justice. The other kings that defeat them are no better. The prophet's bond with power remains under the question mark of the critique of power which is set over against all kingship in the book of Judges: It is only the bramble who volunteers to rule over the trees (Judges 9:7-15).

What remains in all the commotion is the plea of the small still voice which becomes audible after wandering through the desert to Mount Horeb, where the people of Israel, led by Moses, had danced around the Golden Calf, while Moses received the Ten Commandments. This, too, is a situation of utmost ambiguity. What then does it mean to listen to the still small voice, the voice of silence? The silenced voices of people who do not bow before Baal? Bowing to Baal means bowing to militarism, to the powers of war and brute force, the empire builders, the land grabbers who cook up false cases and kill.

It reminds me of the speech of the Home Minister on the occasion of the heightening of Sardar Sarovar Dam, commemorating the three great achievements of this government. Pokhran II, Kargil and the victory in the Supreme Court, to heighten the dam. Dams and bombs vis-a-vis this, there is an email that says that 450 women have congregated at Baba Amte's Ashram to celebrate Narmada Jayanthi and vow to sustain Mother Narmada.

There are several renowned scientists like Dr.Harsh Gupta, Director of the National Geophysical Research Institute and Prof. R.I.Negi of NGRI, who have raised their voice regarding the seismicity of the Narmada-Sone-Lineament which makes the region extremely hazardous for the building of dams. Even theirs is a still small voice in the hum-drum of relief work. The churches today are under pressure to show their Indian pedigree and to demonstrate patriotism. Kargil was such an occasion, the Gujarat earthquake is another one. How do we do it in such a way that the small still voices can be heard?

We are gathered here on the home ground of one of the oldest Christian traditions in the country. What does it mean? Listening to the still small voice raises fundamental questions about our culture. Are we bowing to the priests of Baal or are we prepared to share our life with the widow of Zarephat? We are all the time forced to make such choices. None of these are clear-cut. Are we able to listen to the Dalit President of the Republic who upholds the Constitution and defends the right to life and livelihood of the adivasis? Even his voice at time appears to be small, unheeded. Are we able to listen to the voices of Dalit women like Yashodammal, Indira and Rathnammal of Thiruvalur who are murdered in the struggle against alcoholism? Are we able to hear the voice of Panchavarnam of Round Building in Chennai, who was burnt alive by 40 *goondas* in a Chennai slum in January this year? How then, do we read this text of Kings 19 in our present context?

It is not a matter of one religion against another, because there are Israelites and Sidonites on either side.

It is not a matter of "culture" either in which e.g. a clear-cut feminist position can be taken. Feminist theologians have rightly pointed out the nature sustaining contents of Canaanite religion which the common people, and women in particular, never gave up. But this is a different matter from the militaristic contents of the Baal religion and the difficulty is that in real life all these forces get mixed up with murder. It is only under Elisha that the soldiers are slain with blindness, fed and sent home (2 Kings 6:15-26).

It is not even a matter of "good governance" against "bad governance" because any power struggle requires alliances and alliances require compromises, which are always problematic. But it is necessary to look into what is happening to people's right to life and livelihood and to basic democratic institutions in society and in the church.

It may be a matter of discerning at every step where the spirit of oppression, slavery and servility takes over and where the still small voice gets muffled. We may not be able to still the wind, the fire, the earthquake, they will be there, but God is not in them. We may have our hands full creating spaces where the voices of silence can be heard.

(February 2000)

* * * *

II. OVERCOMING VIOLENCE

30

7. MILITARISM AND PEACE

Judith 4

1. Introduction

Chapter 4 of the book of Judith sets the scene for the spiritual recovery of the people of Israel under the onslaught of Holophernes who is conquering the whole region, advancing towards Judea. Holophernes is supposed to be the Commander-in-chief of King Nebuchadnezzar, King of Assyria. This is all historically very implausible, because Nebukadnezzar is said to have lived from 604-562. Nineveh, where he is supposed to have resided, was already destroyed in 612. But he is also said to have ruled after the return of the people from the Babylonian exile and the restitution of the Jewish cult (520-516).

It is obviously not a historically accurate narrative, but some kind of historical memory was related to it. The story of Judith is similar to the triumphs which are remembered in the song of Deborah (Judges 5). Judith has to be seen in line with Deborah and Jael, a story which is however placed in the period of the Judges, before Israel had settled into kingship.

In contrast to this, the story of Judith is set after return from Exile and restitution of the Jewish cult. Some commentators say it may have been written in the middle of the 2nd century B.C. Thus, the story may also be read in contrast to the story of Esther in which the Jewish religion of Esther remains concealed initially, but where the people of Israel later take extended military revenge. In Judith's story, the faith of Judith is out in the open. She herself takes violent action. However, there is no gloating in the numbers of enemies that have been killed.

It is difficult to decide just how militaristic and chauvinistic this history should be read. There is no way of getting round the cutting off of Holophernes' head and it being carried in a bag in order to make it available for public display. The praise for Judith's beauty, her seductiveness, her chastity - all these appear to be male phantasies which have little in common with what actually happens to women in times of war.

2. Is Judith's God Militaristic?

There are also numerous statements which are directed against a spirit of militancy and which show the people of Israel and their God from a perspective of peace. In ch.5, when Holophernes inquires with Achior, the leader of the Ammonites, what sort of nation is living there in the hill country, he tells the whole history of their different places of settlement, their exile in Egypt and return and says that theirs is a god "who hates wickedness" and that they would be invisible as long as they are faithful to their God (ch.5:18-21). Even more significant, Judith says, (9, 7) "they do not know that thou art the God who stamps out wars" - "the God of the humble, the help of the poor, the support of the weak/ the protector of the desperate/the deliverer of the hopeless (9,11) as well as the ruler of heaven and earth and the creator of the waters" (9, 12).

Victory is attained single handedly by Judith who cuts down Holophernes and who in the end praises God as the one who stamps out war (16:3). This is done by a woman's hand, not a young man's or a Titan's or a giant (16:6,7) and it leads to the triumph of the weak (v.11-12).

In the light of this overview, let us return to chapter 4. Chapter 4 shows the panic of the people in the face of fresh conquest, just after their return to Jerusalem. The situation leads to a sense of despair and penitence. They occupy all the mountain paths but then they do penance. V.10 tells us that they put sackcloth on themselves and everybody else as well as on the altar and implored the God of Israel not to allow their children to be captured, their wives to be carried off, their cities to be destroyed and their temple to be desecrated. The Lord heard their prayer and pitied their distress.

However, the spirit of the people is not valiant throughout. We hear in ch.7 that they get worn out when their water supplies run out and try to make a bargain with the magistrate as it will be better to stay alive as slaves than to perish. Judith comes out in heavy critique against the deadline of five days given in the end of ch.7 and emphasizes that it is not for the people to impose conditions and that God cannot be bargained with (ch.8:14-17).

In the light of all these events, it appears that the objective of the narrative is to scale down the military aspect and to emphasize the aspect of rescuing the desperate, provided the people themselves remain firm in spirit.

3. This leads us to the other important question in this book: Is Judith's God chauvinistic? The totally unbending enmity towards Holophernes and Nebuchadnezzar in this story may lead us to think that the God of Judith is a chauvinistic god who does not tolerate the religion of other

people. This impression is averted by the radical self-questioning of which Joakim, the high priest, leads the people in ch.4. All the people, Jews and foreigners, old and young, men and women, priests and lay, are in sackcloth and ashes even the altar itself is dressed in sackcloth. The enmity against Nebuchadnezzar and Holophernes is not against pagan gods, but against a form of Kingship in which the ruler himself plays God. Nebuchadnezzar himself insists that only he be worshiped by every nation and invoked as a god by men of every tribe and tongue (ch.3, 8).

Some of the commentaries on the book of Judith point to the fact that there is a relationship between the conquest which Holophernes undertakes and the upheavals of wars between different kings in Gen. 4 in which Sodom and Gomorrah get ransacked. Abram rescues his relatives in this chapter and peace is restituted without revenge. This peace is somehow made possible by the participation of Melchizedek, the king of Salem, whose name itself is significant. He is the "King of Justice" and was a priest of God Most High. Melchizedek is the counter-image to Nebuchadnezzar. Abram gives the tithe to Melchizedek after peace has been restored. In the letter to the Hebrews ch.7, Melchizedek is seen as the forerunner of Christ.

Conclusion

While Melchizedek is a counter-image to Nebuchadnezzar, the question how peace can be built is not answered in the book of Judith. Is the solution which the book of Judith projects in any way feasible?

Looking at ch.4, we get the impression that the people are able to overcome the enemy with God's help by collective penance. However, this does not last. We hear in ch.8 that the people cave in under the water scarcity and try to bargain with god. It is in such a situation that Judith volunteers to save the situation. She prays and transforms herself from a sackcloth wearing widow into a seductress.

This leads to an accumulation of different male phantasies: She is a widow and chaste, she is also dazzlingly beautiful and seductive. She is pious and keeps all the rituals, but she also cuts off Holophernes' head and carries it with her in a bag for public display. The collective dimension of penance gets substituted by individual heroism.

While ch.4 says that the people did penance and God heard their prayer and took pity on them, the collective effort to build peace is not pursued in the later chapters of the book of Judith. Individual heroism, be it by women or men, cannot bring peace. The need for the whole community to change into a peaceful society remains as a task ahead.

(November 26, 2001)

* * * *

8. ABEL, RISE UP!

Genesis 4

During the recent weeks and months, we have experienced violence in unprecedented measure. After the murder of municipal councillor Ms.Leelavathi, a large number of murders of women have occurred in the city of Madurai. In the southern districts, caste related violence has been rampant. Only a month age, six dalits were murdered in broad daylight in a bus near Melur. It appears that human life has become cheap. Civil society is breaking down. Is there any way of making people answerable for all the lives lost? When I went to Bombay in a train the other day, I got stuck in a bandh for sixteen hours because ten dalits had been shot by the police. What struck me most was that among the passengers nobody was in fact interested who had been murdered by whom and why. There was no sense of outrage any more.

I would like to go back to the familiar text of Gen.4 in order to raise once again the question: How are we answerable for human life, for human blood?

First of all, there are, from the outset, some marked differences between Cain and Abel. When Cain is born, his mother greets him with the words: I have gotten a man (ish), a male. At the same time, the very name Abel, *haval*, has the meaning: vapour, cloud of dust, nothingness. There is a difference in the occupation as well: Abel grazes sheep while Cain is a tiller of the ground. Cain has control over land while Abel is migrant. Each of them bring an offering. Cain offers the first fruit of the ground and Abel brings the fat parts of the firstlings of the flock. The strange thing which we are told then is that God looks at Abel's offering but not at Cain's. This apparent injustice worries many people. However, the simple explanation probably is that God looks at that which is weak. "God chose what is weak in the world to shame the strong" says Paul in I Cor.1:27.

There is nothing wrong with Cain's offering, Cain has not committed any mistake. But God looks at that which is weak. It is this which makes Cain angry, he loses his temper, he loses face. He cannot master his feelings.

We know this anger from many of the violent incidents mentioned above. If the weak, the women, the dalits, the adivasis, the poor, the uneducated state their point that they are human beings and make a claim to dignity, there is outrage.

It is this anger and loss of face which God questions very directly in v.7. God asks Cain: If you do the right thing, you will have a place of honour. If you do not do right, sin is crouching at the door. It's desire is for you and you must rule over it.

We hear that Cain spoke to his brother but we do not hear what he said. It is not written in the Hebrew text. Since he was angry, he would have run him down. Do you think you are something better? I'll teach you a lesson. We do not hear whether Abel had a reply to this. We only hear that Cain rose up against his brother and killed him. And Cain has no answer to the question: "Where is your brother". Only: "I do not know. Am I my brother's keeper?"

Henceforth, the blood of Abel is crying from the ground and Cain shall be a fugitive and wanderer on earth. Those who appropriate the land violently, cannot keep it. But even though Cain becomes a fugitive, nobody shall be allowed to kill him.

After Cain has become fugitive and dwells East of Eden, we hear of different forms of civilisation which arise from his lineage. He has a son Enoch and builds a city which he calls after Enoch. Enoch has a great grand son Lamech and from Lamech's wives come descendants of different civilizations. Jabal stands for those who live in tents and breed cattle. Jubal is the father of the musicians and Tubal-Cain was a forger of bronze and iron. However, with Lamech the logic of revenge escalates to unimaginable proportions. Lamech will be avenged seventy-seven fold; whoever touches him will be murdered.

But this is not the end of the chapter. In the end of the chapter we hear that Adam knows his wife again and she bears a son "Seth" which means: Substitute. Seth replaces Abel who was slain by Cain. Seth in turn, has a son Enosh. And then the chapter closes. And at that time people began to call upon the name of the Lord. What does this mean? What is the meaning of Enosh? Enosh is a very ancient word which means: Human Being. But it actually means a human being who is weak, miserable, prone to death. In Enosh, the Nothingness of Abel, vapour, who was done away with, rises up to claim his humanity. And people began to call on the name of the Lord. This also means: The Lord could call on people to ask: Where is your brother? Your sister?

How does it happen that those who are weak and prone to be crushed and annihilated claim their humanity in such a way that life can be protected? It is hard to answer this question. I will try to make part of this answer visible in a poem written by a Jewish woman who survived the holocaust.

Abel, rise up
it has to be played afresh
daily it has to be played afresh
daily the answer has to be ahead of us. There must be the option of Yes for an answer
If you do not rise, Abel,
how shall the answer,
the only important answer, ever change itself?

We can close all churches
and abolish all lawbooks
in all the languages of the earth
if only you rise
and undo it
the first wrong answer
to the only question which matters.

Rise up until Cain says
until Cain can say
I am your keeper, brother,
how should I not be your keeper.

Daily rise up
so that we have it ahead of us
this Yes, I am here
I, your brother
until the children of Abel fear no more
because Cain will not be Cain.

I write this a child of Abel
I am daily afraid of the answer
the air in my lungs diminishes
as I wait for the answer.
Abel rise up
So that the beginning changes
(so that it starts differently)
between all of us.
The fires which burn
the fire that burns on Earth
shall be the fire of Abel
and at the tail of the rockets
shall be the fire of Abel.

-    Hilde Domin

May God grant us to be with those who rise up to say Yes
to Life,

Amen.

(August 1, 1997)

* * * *

9. FOLLOWING THE CLOUD
Joshua 24: 1-28

The last chapter of Joshua is not only a brief account of the history before Israelite immigration but also an analysis of what went wrong after the immigration. We find hopelessness as well as hope in it.

The chapter puts before us the whole history of Abraham, Isaac, Jacob and Esau. We come to sense the slavery of Egypt and the journey of liberation undertaken under the leadership of Moses. This was a journey towards Manna (heavenly food), leaving behind the fleshpots of Egypt. Now, the Israelites had entered the land of Canaan, they were settled in urban centers, which they had not built. But they were also surrounded by fertility religion based on agriculture. Will it be possible for them in the new cultural context to remain faithful to the Lord who led them out of Egypt? Do they in fact desire it? Joshua says they are duty-bound to take the decision. They could, if they so desired, worship either the deities left behind by Abraham, Isaac and Jacob on the other side of the river or the gods of Amorites on whose lands they were settled now. Old deities must have been of rivers, trees and the land. The new ones belonged to agricultural resources and urban civilization.

But, the God that Joshua and his family worshipped was different from the above two. He is the God of history; one who transcended time. Jacob had to struggle with the angels of this God to get reconciled with Esau. It was He who gave them the Ten Commandments. But, they left him and started worshipping a golden calf. He only put before them the covenant: "…. I have set before you life and death, blessings and curses. Now choose life, so that you and your children may live … " (Deuteronomy 30:19). Deuteronomy seems to give more hope than the book of Joshua in that it offers a very "simple" choice. We come to know clearly what we must do. The word of God is not something that is above in the sky, distant or beyond the ocean. It is very near in our own mouths and hearts. So, we know what we should do. However, the author of Deuteronomy warned the Israelites that everything would end up in a fiasco, if they did not choose life. "You will not live long in the land you are crossing the Jordan to enter and possess" (Deuteronomy 30:18).

One strong point that emerges is that Joshua was aware that it was impossible to serve the Lord faithfully. Joshua asked the Israelites to choose one God. Accordingly when they chose the God that led them through the journey in the desert, he told them: "You are not able to serve the Lord… If you forsake the Lord and serve foreign gods, he will turn and bring disaster on you and make an end of you … " (Joshua 24: 19,20).

But, when the people insisted: "No! We will serve the Lord" (Joshua 24:21), Joshua said: "You are witnesses against yourselves that you have chosen to serve the Lord ". (verse 22). They replied: "Yes, we are witnesses". (Verse 23) "We will serve the Lord our God and obey him." (Verse 24)

Joshua made a covenant with the people and set up a large stone under the oak tree at the place of worship as a mark of witness. This was to prevent them from sliding back. Then Joshua sent the people away, each to his own inheritance. Joshua dies soon after. Joseph's bones, which the Israelites had brought up from Egypt, were buried at his land of inheritance. There is a passage in the New Testament (Chapter 11 of the book of Hebrews) which is in conflict with the above. Even if people want to, they cannot reach the goal. They may only see what is promised from afar. The history of the Israelites is recollected in all its precariousness. During their migrations, the lives of the Israelites were neither secure nor free from danger. People appeared to be not witnessing the fulfillment of any vow they made. Instead, they were groping in the dark, missing their way and losing their contacts. It was a history full of suffering and failure. Yet, the command to choose life was still valid. Even many witnesses failed in their attempts and got crucified on the cross. It is necessary to see beyond the crisis the light of resurrection.

If we compare our own present life with what is portrayed in these passages, it is really sad that we have not really made a good choice. When I look at the global ecological destruction, I find that our current development policies are creating a situation wherein survival, especially the survival of the poor, is at stake. There does not appear to be any easy alternative to this. Even the poor have no simple alternatives. If a few village communities made an attempt to return to the traditional way of rain-fed agriculture, the government policies would mostly press them down and discourage them. They are not able to return to their traditional deities, rivers and trees or to a life closer to nature. Market ideology makes people fall down and worship it, just as the Israelites worshipped the golden calf. This is the context in which we are called to identify good and evil, life and death. If our choice goes wrong, it becomes clear that death is at hand. Even if we choose the right option, we are likely to lose our way or meet with failure. Again and again we may find ourselves trapped in a situation of crisis. Yet, it is necessary that we make repeated efforts. Then only we will have mental tranquility in the feeling that the cloud of fire will lead us. Many embraced death due to the love that enflamed their hearts like the cloud of fire.

Let us pray for the will to follow the cloud of fire. We too shall glow with the flame of love and thereby get enabled to see beyond the cross the resurrection and the new life.

* * * *

10. LAMENT AND RESURRECTION
Jeremiah 31:15-22

This passage consists of weeping and lamentation. Written during the days of imprisonment, it recalls death and destruction. Yet, it affirms the resurrection that will take place. It envisages new life. We feel aghast at the news of death and destruction reported everyday in the daily newspapers. We have lost our capacity to bear or face death. Many people develop an attitude to drink and make merry, because tomorrow we are dead. We do not even have the strength to feel the agony. Therefore, we lose the capacity to live.

It is comforting that such passages of weeping and lamentation that affirm life are found in the prophetic text. The voice and the metaphor undergo several changes in this passage. First, we hear Rachel, mother of Joseph and Benjamin, weeping for her dead children. "A voice is heard in Ramah, mourning and great weeping, Rachel weeping for her children and refusing to be comforted, because her children are no more" (verse 15). Rachel is the mother of the Israelites. She represents the people of Israel. She is weeping for her lost children.

God hears the wailing voice of Rachel; he consoles her and offers her a hopeful future as it is mentioned in verses 16 and 17. The Lord says:" Restrain your voice from weeping and your eyes from tears, for your work will be rewarded." A mother devotes her life to her children and gives them a good life. But her work often has no value or acceptance in the society. However, God accepts her work. He says, "They (the children) will return from the land of the enemy." While a mother spends all her life to bring up a child, this life could be destroyed in a minute. But, such violent acts will not succeed. God proclaims that only the life – giving work of the woman will succeed.

The people referred to in the passage are portrayed not only as mothers shedding tears but also as indisciplined children. The voice changes to the unruly son "You disciplined me like an unruly calf, and I have been disciplined. Restore me, and I will return, because you are the Lord my God" (verse 18), says Ephraim. The return to the country as well as the come-back to God is indicated here by the Hebrew word *shuv*, which has the connotation of repentance as well as of returning. In the latter part of Deuteronomy 30 : 19, it is said: " .... I have set before you life and death, blessings and curses. Now choose life so that you and your children may live". It points to the return of Ephraim to his country and also to the repentance and the return of Ephraim to God's command.

"Restore me and I will return, because you are the Lord my God" (verse 8). Returning to God may mean facing shame and disgrace, humiliation and blame. The Hebrew word says, "Ephraim beat his thighs." Beating the thighs could be called a drastic symbol of surrender of masculinity, signifying weakness, impotence and vulnerability. This is very much needed for returning to God and the country. This image is devoid of militarism and triumphalism.

The metaphor of God changes in verse 20 in the passage. Like an affectionate and sympathetic mother, God turns to Ephraim. The mother still considers him as a pet child.

"Though I often speak against him, I still remember him. Therefore my heart yearns for him. I have great compassion for him", declares the Lord. The word used for "showing compassion" is showing *rachamim,* the movement of the womb. This love of the movement of the womb makes Ephraim repent and return to God. The movement of the womb is found in several passages of the Old Testament, suggesting the "resurrection of life." In verse 30, chapter 43 of Genesis, it is said that the movement of the womb of Joseph wept for his brother Benjamin. Verse 13 of Psalm 103 tells us about the movement of the womb of God, which signifies his love for his children. Only this affection leads us towards a new life.

This alone makes a connection between the new metaphors in verses 21 and 22. The Israelites are now represented in the metaphor of a virgin. Now, Rachel is not a mother, nor Ephraim a child. The young, inexperienced and vulnerable woman is vested with the responsibility of reading signposts and exploring paths. The woman becomes one that will guide the journey of life. Even if she is reluctant to guide, God encourages her to do so. He says, "How long will you wander, O unfaithful daughter? The Lord will create a new thing on earth - a woman will surround a man." There is again a change of metaphor in this last sentence. The words used here are very direct. The word indicating the woman expresses the meaning of "the penetrated one" or "the one who is captured through an act of sex". The virgin has lost her virginity. But she has gained power and experience. The word indicating the man signifies the characteristics of "masculinity", "power", "wealth" and "violence." Only the woman, "who has the power of producing life", can surround and protect the male from heading for destruction. By sensing the movement of the womb, men can learn to love and be affectionate. This is an act newly created by God.

We, who have reflected on the passage, find it difficult to acknowledge this. Since violence and death rule this world, it becomes difficult to be loving and affectionate. It is even more difficult to think that things will change. I would like to cite a few recent violent incidents. Professor Rajini Rajasingham, one of the founding members of University Teachers for Human Rights (UTHR) in Jaffna, who courageously exposed human rights violations of the Sinhala Army, the IPKF and of different militant groups, was brutally murdered on 21st September 1989. She condemned all human rights violations, be it of the Sinhalese Army, of the Indian Peace Keeping Force or of the militant liberationists. She desired that all murders and violations of right to life must be ended. She was killed for the very same reason.

I would also like to remind you about the killing of Muthupillai of Meenakshipuram on 9th September, which was followed by a series of murders in the area. We must promote movements that see to it that justice is really done without such cases getting appropriated for narrow political ends.

I must also refer here to the death of Ms.Leela Joyce, lecturer of Sarah Tucker College, who was abused and murdered in her marital home and is described by her friends as a dedicated teacher, a loving friend and a joyful colleague. Her associates say: "The link in the chain got broken all of a sudden, and the bird flew away to a safe place." We need to take responsibility for the situation of women being not in a position to live peacefully.

Violence is not only expressed in individual acts of rape or murder. It is not confined to warfare either. It can also take the route of "development". I want to keep in mind the tens of thousands of Adivasis, who assembled at Harsoot in M.P on 28th September. They were all displaced from their original habitats due to the construction of the Narmada Dam. Their town will go under shortly. Also, there was a rally in Nagercoil recently against Koodankulam Nuclear Reactor. Imagine, the technology is acquired from the Soviet Union, which only five years ago had the most severe nuclear accident in human history.

It requires a lot of effort to arrest the powers that destroy life in the name of development and growth. If we realize our mistake and get involved in efforts to affirm life, we have the promise of God that the power to destroy life could be crushed and life could succeed. Let us pray to God to give us the will to bear with disgraces and to take responsibility. We must have the wisdom to choose life for the sake of having the will to grieve over deaths that happen beyond our control and to confront and prevent violence wherever we can.

(October, 1989)

* * * *

11. PEACE IN THE CONTEXT OF VIOLENCE

Micah 4:1-5 & Revelation 21:1-5

How can we speak about peace in the context of violence? We do not even have proper words to use. 'Samathanam' and 'amaithi' do not convey, because they have a connotation of quietness. "Peace of Mind", which seems to stem from closing one's eyes and looking inward. But we are conscious of enormous violence over the past years; the bombing of Afghanistan, after September 11, 2001; then the carnage in Gujarat after February 28, 2002; then the Second Gulf War. Besides, we know that there is no day or night in which women are not raped or murdered, even in their own houses. Names like Kizhvenmani or Melevalavu are symbols of unthinkable violence against Dalits. The rising floods in the Narmada Valley are taking away the houses and fields of thousands of Adivasis. We have to open our eyes to the ongoing violence in society. How can we speak of peace? We can use the word, "wholeness" or *nirai vazhvu, meyvazhvu,* in which case we come closer to the word "Shalom" in Hebrew. However, we feel uncertain about Hebrew as well, because it reminds us of the situation in today's Jerusalem, where Israelis and Palestinians are making contesting claims on the holy places. In today's world, there are two places which are close to the possibility of nuclear war. Israel vis-a-vis the Palestinians and its Arab neighbours and India vis-a-vis Pakistan.

It is a strange irony that both the texts which describe peace visions, given for today's Sunday, are centred around Jerusalem and the Zion. I want to mainly focus on the text from the prophet Micah. The peace vision in chapter 4 is a familiar text. But it stands in stark contrast with the devastating critique against false prophets in chapter 3. The false prophets cry "Peace" when they have something to eat, but declare war against him who puts nothing into their mouth (3:5). Therefore, the people will be in dark night, without vision. God will give no answer. Only Micah is full of spirit. He cries out to the rulers (3:9-12) who abhor justice and destroy equity, who build Zion with blood and Jerusalem with wrong. Jerusalem's heads give judgement for bribe, the priests teach for hire, the prophets divine for money. Yet they lean upon the Lord and say. "Is not the Lord in the midst of us? No evil shall come upon us. Therefore, because of you, Zion shall be ploughed like a field. Jerusalem shall become a heap of ruins, and the mountain of the Lord a wooded height".

Micah criticizes in chapter 3 that Jerusalem has been "built with blood". In this time, Jerusalem had become a mighty fortress with big walls and storehouses. There had also been the building of a tunnel, to bring the water of the Gichon spring into the inner city, a construction of 512m, length. Contractors must have made lots of money. It is such economic growth, which has brought corruption. The whole justice system was subverted (as we know from Is.1:23 and 5:23). The poor, the widows and orphans cannot expect justice in this situation. It is because of this total subversion of justice that God had fallen silent and Jerusalem is destined to fall in ruins, to be ploughed as an open ground, left to become wilderness, a haunt for wild animals.

This image of destruction in the time of Micah is likely to belong to the second half of the eighth century, a time of consolidation and expansion of kingship and urbanization. This is indeed followed by the Babylonian exile and the dominance of the Persians. The destruction comes true. But chapter 4, in total contrast has a vision of peaceful reconstruction, which is extraordinary in its power. While Micah from the town of Moreshet very courageously takes on the false prophets, he is also connected with this vision of peace. The same text as in Micah 4:1-3 can also be found in Is.2:2-4, one century later. Some commentaries believe that these visions of peace, which are further developed in chapters 4-6 of the book Micah, are composed later, after the Exile, perhaps after the reconstruction of the temple, towards the end of the 6th century B.C. This is difficult to decide. Often we think that the prophets only expressed criticism and predicted disaster. How could the prophet have thought of the return of the nations to Zion after announcing the total destruction of Zion due to exploitation and corruption. We do not know.

But we know one thing and that is: It only makes sense to speak of peace in the midst of violence itself, because without facing and acknowledging the depth of violence, peace is only a privilege and a self-deception, it is not for the common people, the poor, the oppressed.

Thus, having acknowledged the violence and the corruption and self-deception of the false prophets, let us now look at the vision of peace. The verses 1-4 are expressing four steps: First of all, the mountain of the house of the Lord shall be raised above all hills. Secondly, the nations shall flock to that hill. It is they who take the initiative, not God himself or his prophets. It is the nations themselves who say, let's go up to the mountain of God that he may teach his ways and we may walk in his path. This is possible, because from Zion shall go out the Torah, the law of God and the word of God from Jerusalem. He shall judge among many peoples and shall decide for strong nations afar off.

Thirdly, there is as a result, a peace initiative among the nations, which is nothing short of a miracle; they shall beat their swords into ploughshares and their spears into pruning hooks. The arms become agricultural implements. The people start growing food instead of killing each other. They shall no longer learn warfare, they shall forget how one kills, rapes and bombs.

Fourthly, instead, they shall sit under their fig tree and their vine. "Everyman", it is said. But of course, "every woman" must also find a place of rest, because the purpose of this rest is that "no one shall make them afraid" the Lord of hosts has spoken. It is only here that Micah uses the term Zebaoth, in the rest of the text, even the name, the tetragrammaton, is hardly used, except in combinations like, "the mountain of the house of the Lord", "the word of the Lord".

After this in verse 5, comes yet another statement, which is unique to the text in Micah and does not occur in Isaiah: "All the peoples walk each in the name of its god, but we will walk in the name of the Lord our God for ever and ever".

This seems to suggest that, though the nations come to Zion, to be guided by the Torah and to learn peace and unlearn war, they do not change their religion. They come each with their god. The whole text never mentions Israel and uses the name of God only very sparingly. There is no victory, conversion or surrender to only one God. Peace is only thinkable with cultural pluralism and a voluntary decision to unlearn war.

Can we learn from this? Can we learn to muster courage to denounce injustice and exploitation where we encounter it? Can we learn to identify consumerism, corruption, opportunism as the root of injustice? Can we overcome the self-righteousness of the false prophets? Can we recognize the silence of God even while we think we have him in our pocket, like the Bible? And can we think peace? Can we think how to un-learn war? Can we think of the nations coming to learn peace, each with their own god? Can we think of bringing up our children in such a way that they un-learn war? How? Put off the TV? Stop beating in our houses? Arrange mixed marriages? Join a peace movement? Build one? Share house-work? I think we all have to discusss and decide, again and again.

I would like to think of this vision in Micah also at a symbolic level. The Zion in this vision becomes the highest mountain; it is a guiding light to the nations who come to learn peace. As such, the Zion is a counter-image to the tower of Babel which pits the nations against each other in a confusion of languages. At the same time, the nations come each in the name of their God. While the tower of Babel has to do with a feverish competition about "who is the greatest", the vision in Micah is related to agriculture, freedom from violence, not being raided and plundered.

The rest under the fig tree and the vine has an element of contemplation, side by side with the element of physical labour, which is very different from the stern prophetic voice of Micah in chapter 3. This contemplation is also related with the movement of the nations towards the center.

Holy mountains and holy rivers need to be circumbulated. Often the center of the circle is considered to be feminine, while the out-ward movement is considered to be masculine. In ancient Canaan there were many fertility goddesses which dwelled on hilltops and in trees. In many prophetic books we hear of the destruction of the fertility cults, including the book of Micah. However, in the peace vision of Micah 4, the nations come each with their god, they may come with their goddess. There is space for healing a broken history. Or so we hope.

Let me close with a brief reflection on the text of Revelation 21:1-5 where we hear that the New Jerusalem comes down out of heaven, adorned like a bride, for her husband, the lamb. The striking thing in this vision is the direct presence of God with his people; "He will dwell with them and they shall be his people, and God himself will be with them" (21:3). When this happens, tears will be wiped away and an end to death, pain and mourning will come. Again, we do not hear of a temple. God dwells directly with his people. The promise is: Behold, I make all things new.

There is one thing which is deeply problematic in Revelation and likewise in the prophetic texts of the first testament. Good women are virgins or wives, bad women are whores. The most saintly thing to be achieved is a virgin mother, motherhood without sexuality. This requires to split women up into "good women" - those who are under control - and "bad women" whose are "lose" - morally as well as in the head.

It is such compartmentalisation of women, such appropriation of women, which leads to the pretext of "freeing the women of Afghanisthan from the Taliban", while in reality it's all about oil. It is this which leads to the mass rapes in Gujarat after Godhra.

If peace is not just amaithi (stillness), but muzhumai (wholeness) and niraivazhvu (fullness), then we will truly have to think how to make all things new. We may have to change many of our habits and attitudes. We may have to work again and again on our day to day relationships. It may be very disturbing to have to do that. It may undermine our peace of mind, it may be strenuous. We may have to disturb the peace of patriarchy. But we cannot expect that "learning peace" and "not learning war anymore" is simple. May we have the courage and perseverance to keep trying. Amen.

(August 24, 2003)

* * * *

III. RESURRECTION AND UPRISING

12. WISDOM WILL BE JUSTIFIED BY HER DEEDS

Matthew 11:12-19

This text speaks of a situation of tension. The new life of the Kingdom of God which Jesus announces in the Gospel of Matthew has already begun, but people do not understand what is going on. John the Baptist is in jail. He himself has sent messengers (Matt.11:2ff) to inquire whether Jesus is the one whose coming John announces. Jesus only answers: "The blind see, the lame walk, the lepers are cleansed, the deaf hear and the dead are raised up, the poor have good news preached to them and blessed is he who takes no offence at me".

There is a great closeness between Jesus and John the Baptist. At the same time, Jesus and John are also worlds apart. Jesus makes clear that John is a prophet. John has called people forcefully to repent and renew their life. He himself looks desperate. Jesus calls him "A reed shaken by the wind". He preaches in the desert, he wears dress of camel hair. He is a loner, a man of harsh words.

Jesus too is not known as a soft person. In the preceding chapter we find the saying: I have not come to bring peace, but the sword. He sets sons and fathers, daughters and mothers, daughters-in-law and mothers-in-law, against each other. But at the same time, Jesus is known as the one who heals the sick, feeds the hungry and moves with tax collectors and sinners.

How can we understand these contradictions? While John calls people to repent and lives an ascetic life, Jesus expresses the fullness of life. He breaks through the separations in society. He mixes with women. He heals on the Sabbath. He moves from a position where he considers himself as come only for the lost sheep of Israel, to a position where non-Jews are also integrated and accepted. While the disciples try to get rid of the Canaanite woman who shouts after them, Jesus gets dragged into an argument with her and finally attests her "great faith" (Matt. 15:21-28).

The new life does not come spectacularly. The skies do not open with lightning and thunder, no curtain rises for the first act of the Kingdom of God. The new life starts by touching lepers, moving around with hungry crowds, admitting shouting women and squealing children. It is an utterly strenuous, tiresome organisational process. Many times we hear that Jesus "retreats" when the situation becomes critical. But the crowds know to find him.

In this situation which is full of expectation, there is also ample scope for violence. Men of violence are taking power by force. There were many groups at the time who were prepared to counter the political powers by an armed uprising. They thought that they could hasten the coming of the Kingdom of God by armed struggle.

Jesus, on the contrary, claims that the new life has already started. It cannot be "hastened" by artificial means. Jesus confirms that John the Baptist is the prophet Elijah whom the Jews expected to go ahead of the Messiah. But John is in jail, not a very attractive option. He is later killed in jail. At the same time, Jesus lives a life which is also not all that attractive.   He is endlessly on the move, surrounded by crowds. But he not only feeds the hungry, he himself likes to eat and drink and celebrate. We often do not like to face this.   Jesus is heavily criticised for eating with tax collectors and sinners and not keeping the fasts of the Pharisees. (Matt. 9:14-17). He justifies his lifestyle with the new life which has started. But people find this difficult to understand. Jesus is dismayed over their response.   He says: To what shall I compare this generation. You are like children in the marketplace, unable to agree what to play. They will accuse each other: We have piped, but you have not danced.   We have wailed but you have not beaten your breast.   They can only quarrel. No one is clear what they want to do.

But Jesus concludes very simply: "Wisdom will be justified by her deeds".   He himself identifies with the female figure of wisdom here.

Wisdom as a female emanation of God is not familiar to us. We do not usually speak of her in the church. But she was familiar to Jesus. Wisdom is not about "know-ledge", something intellectual and abstract. She is, in the first place, the force which affirms life itself: "Do not invite death by the error of your Life, or bring destruction by the work of your hands; because God did not make death and he does not delight in the death of the living. For he created all things so that they might exist" (Wisdom of Sol. Ch.1:12-14a). We have heard in the readings (Jesus Sirach 4:11+14a) what Wisdom does, "Wisdom teaches her children and gives help to those who seek her. Whoever loves her, loves life, and those who seek her from early morning are filled with joy".

Wisdom exhorts: Do not be ashamed to be yourself. Those who blame Jesus of being a glutton and a drunkard, moving with shady characters, try to make him ashamed of himself. But wisdom says: There is a shame that is glory and favour. That which appears as a scandal in the eyes of the moralists, is glory and favor. Following wisdom implies taking risks. Wisdom goes on to exhort: Do not refrain from speaking at the proper moment and do not hide your wisdom. Never speak against the truth, but be ashamed of your ignorance.

If we stand up for the truth of a contested cause, our adversaries will poke holes into our argument. The struggle about the Narmada dams shows this at the national level. Is there land, is there no land? Can people be resettled and live or can they live where they are and still there will be enough water? How much is enough? For whom, For what?

These verses sound like they were designed for the Narmada struggle. They should be read out in the Supreme Court: "Never speak against the truth, but be ashamed of your ignorance. Do not be ashamed to confess your sins and do not try to stop the current of a river. Do not subject yourself to a fool or show partiality to a ruler. Fight to the death for Truth and the Lord God will fight for you" (J. Sirach 4: 25-28).

This was the situation in the time of Jesus and it is the situation today. We are used to speaking of Jesus' death and resurrection in doctrinal terms. But if we face the waters, standing in them upto the waist or to the neck for 14 hours or 30 hours, death is cruelly close by, and resurrection looks very remote.

We are facing controversial situations in many places: In Chidambaram district the polls have been rigged. Houses have been burnt and children cannot go to school and have no drinking water. But repolling is refused. We are facing this situation where 21 Dalits are sentenced under National Security Act in a murder case "to state an example" but the murderers of Madurai Councillor Leelavathy and of Panchayat President Murugesan and his five associates in Melevalavu, have not been arrested. It appears to be a very desperate situation, but it is not more desperate than what Jesus went through in his lifetime.

It is important not to harden in this situation and not to get desperate, lest the Kingdom of God should suffer violence. It is also important not to become cynical and find fault with everything and everybody like those children on the market place. We are called to celebrate life whole heartedly whenever we can and we are allowed to mourn whole heartedly whenever we suffer losses. We have to be clear about the next step and full of courage and patience. We are encouraged to learn from the call of wisdom which Jesus exclaims at the end of this chapter:

> "Come to me all who labour and are heavy laden for I will give you rest. Take my yoke upon you, and learn from me, for I am gentle and lowly in heart, and you will find rest for your souls. For my yoke is easy, and my burden is Light" (Matt. 11:28-29).

Amen.

Special Song:

I have played the flute
in the market place the flute
but of those who have heard
no one danced with me.
I have played the flute
Now, of you who have heard,
who will dance with me.

1. I filled the empty nets with fishes
    till they were bursting
    I fed the crowds with bread and fishes
    hungry and thirsting.

Chorus...

2. I took away the fear of freedom
    from my disciples
    I have restored a heart of wisdom
    to Magdelena

Chorus...

3. I have relieved the heart of sages
    from all their prudence
    Those who have had no work nor wages
    joined in my dancing.

(October 10, 1999)

* * * *

13. FREEDOM AND SLAVERY AFTER POKHRAN

Galatians 5:1-26

Chapter five of Galatians deals in fundamental ways with the topic of freedom and counterposes it to slavery. This is clearly expressed in v.1 of the chapter. Further, the chapter deals with the dichotomy of spirit versus the flesh. This can easily lead to a moralistic reading of the chapter. In an individualistic perspective, it can be presumed that too much freedom leads to licentiousness and immorality, fornication, impurity, (v.19) and thus, a spirituality which is an enemy to the body, asceticism and puritanism can be preached.

However, this is not what this chapter is all about. If we read this text in its historical context, it becomes clear that this chapter makes an attempt to speak about a new community which is free from casteism, communalism and patriarchal subordination. We often quote Galatians 3:28 out of context. In Christ no Jew nor Greek, no master nor slave, no male nor female. But we fail to understand the depth of the attempt to live the new community. This is what the community of Galatia had to struggle with. How to live in freedom and yet preserve cultural identities. The verses 2-12 are dealing with the problem of the circumcision. This refers to a situation in which Christians of Jewish origin and of Greek origin were living together and the question arose how much of the Jewish heritage needed to be upheld among new converts. This was a fundamental question of the relationship between Jews and Greeks in the Galatian Church. If circumcision was practiced, then the whole Torah needed to be kept. Circumcision was a sign of the covenant between God and his people. This had been expressed strongly in Gen.17:10-14 where the alternative is: either circumcision or being uprooted from the people of Israel. We hear in Gen.17 that Abraham circumcises Ishmael, his son from the slave woman Hagar. All the slaves in his house, even those bought from foreigners, were circumcised with Abraham and Ishmael. Only after this, Isaac is born to Sarah as a result of the promise of God. Isaac is not born "according to the flesh". Isaac comes from the promise of God, despite Sarah's infertility. In modern language we speak of surrogate motherhood. But Isaac's birth transcends such physical limitations. Isaac's birth is not "according to the flesh". The patriarchal values of virility and female fertility are completely suspended here. Isaac is born as a practical joke of God. Sarah herself laughs when she hears she will bear a son, it's a truly ridiculous proposal. And this laughter is the origin of Isaac's name.

If Sarah is counterposed to Hagar in Galatians, Ch.4, this is not because she as a free woman is better than the slave woman. On the contrary, Sarah herself was trying to solve the problem of her barrenness "according to the flesh" by providing a surrogate womb from the slave woman. Sarah herself dealt with Hagar in harsh ways out of insecurity and drove her away with her child into the desert (Gen.16:6). Sarah stands for God's desire to break through the limitations of age and sex and solutions of such problems by using a slave woman, or going for any other technical solution. While Sarah's own behaviour remains according to the flesh, God's action with Sarah breaks through this limitation. This is why Sarah stands as a symbol of the spirit of freedom. God makes her to live something which she had not been inclined to believe she could live. She is made to live the spirit of utopia, of that which has no place in the existing society. What Paul misses completely in Chapter 4 of Galatians is the promise which has been given to Hagar while she is pregnant with Ishmael. Ishmael shall bring forth a multitude of people. His very name means: "God has heard" the affliction of the slave woman Hagar. Hagar, too, lives something she did not think she could live. The problem between two women pitted against each other in a competition of producing sons and of master and slave is not resolved. This problem remains in the actual story of Hagar and Sarah. It stays on in the interpretation of Paul. But Paul wrestles with the problem what the leaving behind of slavery and ethnic identity may mean.

In Gal.5:2-12, Paul tries to explain why circumcision is no longer needed. In v.1-6 he argues that the practicing of the whole of the Torah is not feasible for non-Jewish converts. In V.7-12 he tries to argue with those who are trying to uphold the circumcision.

Those who try to uphold the circumcision are people who were influenced by the Zealots. The Zealots felt that only an armed uprising against the colonial power could help Israel to restore its cultural and religious identity. In modern language we could say that these are the fundamentalists. They played identity politics. A Christian community in which Jews and non-Jews simply lived together was not thinkable for them. Multi-cultural identities were considered a threat. So they insisted on the circumcision and the total fulfillment of the Torah. Obviously, under such circumstances the new community could not grow. This is why Paul intervenes.

It appears, the confrontation is quite aggressive. The minority who tries to stand up for freedom and for the risk of faith to live a new life, is under duress. They get intimidated and threatened. The apostle appeals to faith and love (v.6) but the adversaries are trying to impose their legalistic stand. Paul appeals to uphold the scandal of the cross. We are reminded of the violence of fundamentalist positions and the vulnerability of those who try to live sisterhood in the face of such violence. We all know of the anguish in communal riots when circumcision or the wearing of a *bindi* or particular clothes is taken as a sign of communal identity and could become a matter of life and death. In the letter to the Galatians, Paul tries to overcome an identity politics which makes culture, language, ethnicity a matter of life and death and which leads to ethnic cleansing. He exhorts the people to take the risk of insecurity. He demands the courage to live with uncertainties.

However, it is in this same context that Paul also warns against "using the freedom as an opportunity for the flesh". What does this mean in the context of this chapter? The key verses are 13 and 14 which read: "For you were called to freedom, brethren, only do not use your freedom as an opportunity for the flesh, but through love be servants to one another. For the whole law is fulfilled in one word. You shall love your neighbour as yourself". The underlying danger is expressed instantly in v.15: "If you bite and devour one another take heed that you are not consumed by one another". If we follow fundamentalist rules, a pressure is created which enforces unity. If freedom is allowed, there can be factionalism, rivalry, backbiting, enmity, bullying. What is required is serving each other in love. This is not easy. The spirit of freedom requires that we take sides and stand by our convictions. This leads to polarisation. The spirit of love requires that we serve one another. But such service cannot be in a spirit of servility, this too has to be rooted in the spirit of freedom. It is important to relate this back to the question of cultural identity from which this chapter started. If the fundamentalist uniform ethic is rejected, there can be a war of identities. Communalist claims to unity can be undermined by a war of sub-castes. This is not the spirit of freedom which Paul has in mind.

Another way of interpreting the spirit of freedom can be by giving it a consumerist connotation. Let us eat and make merry for tomorrow we are dead. This consumerism can take all sorts of forms.

People can consume sex or religion, following their passions. They can take to superstition, try to practice magic, exhaust themselves in competition, anger, selfishness, party spirit and envy. The tension which this creates again may lead to addiction to alcohol and sex. Despite this text being so old we can easily recognise some very modern connotations in it. This is because the hellenistic philosophy had notions of universalism which fostered a cosmopolitan spirit.

It was the kind of cosmopolitanism which went along with colonialism, slavery and crosses for slaves who staged an uprising against the Roman Empire. In contrast to this, the Jews preserved their very specific history of the Exodus from slavery in Egypt led by Moses. Moses himself as a baby had been saved by a multi-ethnic team of the Hebrew mid wives Shiphrah and Puah, his own sister Miryam and Pharoah`s daughter who brought him up at the Egyptian court. Yet, Israel preserved its own specific history, but is also in danger, of being distorted in a zealotic spirit.

We are directed back towards the basic topics of this chapter and of the letter to the Galatians as a whole: freedom vs. slavery and spirit vs. flesh. The licentiousness of the flesh is not only addicted to physical comforts, it also tries to claim such comforts in forms of collective egoism in the form of family, caste, community. The biting and devouring one another of which we hear can take different forms. It can take the form of fundamentalism against freedom. It can also take the form of corruption and nepotism, each group looking after their own interests, giving jobs to their own relatives, asserting their own way of doing things. It is against this state of affairs that Paul speaks of the "desires of the spirit", which go against the desires of the `flesh`. The desires of the flesh are directed towards material advantage. However, the answer is not denial of will and desire, asceticism. What does Paul mean by the "desires of the spirit": He speaks of the "fruits of the spirit" as love, joy, peace, patience, kindness, faithfulness, self-control.

This may all look meek and mild and a little bit boring as long as we see it in individualistic ways and removed from the background of ethnic rivalries and fundamentalist competition.

I would like to take a bold step and translate this text directly into the situation in the sub-continent after the test explosions of Pokhran II.

We are faced today with a situation of rising communalism and fundamentalism. This is the other side of the universalism of consumerism which characterises globalisation. It leads to a rise in violence between nations, between religions and castes and against women. Many forces play out identity politics against globalisation. Creating external and internal enemies helps to foster an artificial unity. Yet, factions keep biting and devouring one another. During the national conference of the IAWS in Pune a massive march was held against nuclear bombs by 700 people, most of them women, supported by 14 local organisations. It was a silent march with many posters winding its ways through the thoroughfares of consumerism. Pune is a city with lots of army quarters and also a home to Hindu chauvinist organisations. But we all marched fearlessly in the spirit of love, joy, peace, patience, kindness, goodness, faithfulness, gentleness and self-control. Against these, indeed, there is no law. There was no asceticism. Some posters read: Make love, not war. But the people walking there had crucified the flesh in the sense that they did not do this for gain or advantage, they did not think that security comes from arms. They were determined not to be divided by caste, religion, gender, language. They were determined not to succumb to fear and violence. They were determined to see visions and dream dreams of a new society. May we have the courage to reap such fruits of the spirit in our daily lives.   Amen.

(July 30, 1998)

* * * *

14. CHOOSE LIFE !
Deuteronomy 30:15-20

This text is put into the mouth of Moses leading the people of Israel from slavery in Egypt into the promised land. It refers to the Deuteronomic law which is also called the covenant of Moab (Dt.29:1) which is distinct from the covenant on Mount Horeb. This text was written shortly before the period of the Babylonian exile during a reform period in the history of Israel. The deuteronomic law addressed itself to the growing class conflicts in Israel, indebtedness, land alienation. The special sense of urgency came from the fact that the Northern Kingdom had collapsed under the onslaught of the Assyrians. Ten tribes had disappeared into Assyria never to return to the land. The remaining two tribes - Juda and Benjamin - were struggling with the social reforms which were necessary if the will of God was to be implemented - the vision of a society of prosperity and social justice. They had come to know the arbitrariness of rulers, coups and counter-coups, the agonising long rule of Manasse. They had seen the disaster in the North and they were prepared to make an effort to "choose life" as the text says. Actually their reform collapsed, the Babylonian exile could not be avoided. But the school of reformers worked out their ideas in the deuteronomic work of history for future generations to ponder.

In the announcement of today's service, International Peace Day was mentioned. Actually, we just commemorated Hiroshima Day on 6th of August. The 9th of August belongs to Nagasaki. On 6th of August, "Little Boy", a nuclear bomb of 12.5 million kilo tonnes of TNT was dropped on Hiroshima and on 9th August, "Fat Man", a second nuclear bomb of 22 million kilo tonnes of TNT was dropped on Nagasaki. We have commemorated these events with special zeal this year because of Pokhran two, the nuclear tests on May 11th in the Rajasthan Desert and because of Chagai Hills where the nuclear tests were carried out by Pakistan on May 28th. Suddenly, Hiroshima does not seem to be far away any more.

I need not go into the events 53 years ago, the flash, the pressures, the ball of fire, the mushroom cloud, the lakhs of people who died instantly and the lakhs who died an agonising, slow death due to leukemia and other cancers, for decades to come. People from Hiroshima have come to visit Pokhran very shortly after the explosions and they have travelled the country and witnessed the agony of nuclear war all over the country. Here in Madurai, many organisations conducted Hiroshima Day. American College students had a hall meeting and a human chain. Leaflets of National Alliance of People's Movements were distributed to the public in different places. A hall meeting was held by NAPM in SOCO Trust. In many others of the big cities like Delhi, Mumbai, Chennai, major agitations took place.

I would like to reconnect all these events to the text in Deuteronomy 30. First of all, it is important to understand that the major violent disasters in history do not come out of the blue. Nor do people's interventions in history to give society a turn for the better come out of the blue. These interventions are long drawn processes as well. We have to choose life again and again on a day to day base.

Historical failures and crimes revisit us over generations. The people of Israel in the time of Josia when this reform movement for a new and just society started, had suffered for many years under the misrule of his father Manasse who was a vasal of the Assyrians, and who condoned slavery and exploitation, temple prostitution and a total neglect of the ethos of liberation which was enshrined in the memory of the exodus from slavery of the people of Israel. The breakdown of the social fabric which came with the Babylonian exile, had been prepared for long due to foreign collaboration, corruption, selfishness and blind power struggles.

We cannot forget that Japan, which suffered the bombardments at the end of second world war, had been an ally of fascist Germany under Hitler. Not only that, Japan herself had invaded so many countries of South East Asia and kept people in murderous concentration camps. This of course, in no way justifies the nuclear bombs but it explains the war constellation due to which lakhs of innocent people lost their lives in the most unimaginable ways.

However, the nation which authorised the bombing, is known to have built its 200 years of capitalist history on the genocide of the indigenous American Indian population, a history which has never been atoned. It is the nation who was later defeated by the determined people of Vietnam when the US tried to burn them into oblivion with Napalm.

Our own country, with a history of wars in 1947, 1962 (China), 1965 (Pakistan) and 1971 (Bangladesh) is at present ruled by a government which is dominated by communal forces who relate very directly to the heritage of Nazi Germany. This is very frightening because it connects us directly with the history of genocide and of the holocaust. This is very difficult to face. Many people prefer not to admit to themselves or to others that this fascist history stares us in the face. We try to pretend as if we do not know, as if there is a difficulty to assess the circumstances. This, too, is a normal phenomenon under fascism. People prefer to say that they do not know what is happening, that they haven't got enough information to assess the situation.

It is in this situation that the text of Deut.30 chases us out of our comfortable hiding places by saying: "See, I have set before you this day life and good, death and evil". The choices are very clear. The people can follow God's commandments and ordinances, loving God and walking in his ways. In this case they shall live and multiply in the promised land, or they can turn away and worship other Gods and perish.

What does this mean? In the Christian churches we often see idolatry in a very narrow way as if it is a matter of demarcating ourselves as sharply as possible from the surrounding cultures. Even Israel in its history in Canaan was facing this problem. In the process, many precious features of people's culture have been lost and our faith has got alienated from the Earth, from water, from trees, from the cosmos, from life itself. The real danger of idolatry lies somewhere else, in the worship of money and power, greed and exploitation, in the worship of security, of weapons. We cannot serve God and Mammon. Where your treasure is, there is your heart. So we have to ask ourselves what it is that we treasure. The VHP wanted to build a Shakti temple in Pokhran and distributed the irradiated sand as *prasatham*. They told us that the Buddha had smiled again. All this is a sacrilege on Hindu, Buddhist and Dalit culture.

Of course, those forces in our country who have welcomed the bomb and who argue that we need it for our "defence" do not admit that they serve the forces of death. They do not admit that the ensuing arms race will kill us even if these arms are never deployed. If we go for weaponisation our military budget will double. While social spending has already drastically been cut under globalisation, it will be totally unaffordable in the future.

There is no escape route left for us. "For this commandment which I command you this day is not too hard for you, neither is it far off. It is not in heaven that you should say: 'who will go up for us to heaven, and bring it to us, that we may hear it and do it?' Neither is it beyond the sea, that you should say, 'who will go over the sea for us, and bring it to us, that we may hear it and do it'. But the word is very near you; it is in your mouth and in your heart, so that you can do it" (v.11-14).

The word is near to us, it is in our mouth and in our heart. There are no two ways about it. Not only that, God's appeal is made very public. Heaven and earth are called to witness. "I call heaven and earth to witness against you this day, that I have set before you Life and Death, blessing and curse, therefore choose life, that you and your descendents may live, loving the Lord your God, obeying his voice and cleaving to him; for that means life to you and length of days that you may dwell in the land which the Lord swore to your father, to Abraham, Isaac and Jacob, to give them".

What does it mean to choose life? It first of all means *to choose insecurity and vulnerability*. The present logic is one based on deterrence, creating fears, creating enemies, outside and inside and then arming ourselves with means of protection, bombs outside and draconian laws like the POTA inside. Security based on fear is suicide in installments.

Secondly, it means *resurrection and uprising against the forces of death*. We have to awaken from the suicidal mentality which says: Anyway, we all have to die. This perverted bravery which takes the other side into the grave as well, the suicide bomber mentality in the nuclear age is the end of God's good creation itself. There is nothing but resurrection and uprising against this ultimate form of death which denies the right to life to all future generations of living beings except the cockroaches.

Thirdly, we have to *choose life each day* afresh and enter the tedious process of undoing the organised madness which has caught hold of our society bit by bit. In this we have to learn from Dalits who, despite centuries of attack and persecution have been persistent in rebuilding their lives in close proximity with their enemies. We have to resist the ethos of militarisation and build an ethos of repentance and forgiveness. We do this together with millions of other human beings all over the globe who are building peace movements, in India, in Pakistan, in Bangladesh, in Sri Lanka, in Japan, in the US, in Russia. If we want to witness to the resurrection, we can only do so by building Peace Movements for Social Justice and Democracy and against the arms race. Choose Life! Amen.

Let us stand for a moment and remember the dead of the wars, the nuclear tests, uranium mining, communal and caste clashes and other forms of violence.

REQUIEM
(After Chernobyl)

My soul a bird on rainy roof
Cries out in lonely pain
Remembering all who went for good
And will not come again.

Remember those who die their lives
For lack of daily bread
Remember all who live their death
For years and years ahead.

Remember all who face their end
From rays in rains and dust
Who live their lives forever signed
Yet live for life they must.

Somewhere afar a brimful jug
Of love and hope and time
Poured out into each parched heart
To overflow again.

(August 8, 1998)

* * * *

15. THE WOMAN WHO QUESTIONED JESUS

Matthew 15: 21-28, Mark 7: 24-30

Voice 1

The story of the Canaanite or Syro-phoenician woman is often seen as an example for the ministry to be done among the gentiles. It is explained that Jesus went to Tyre and performed this miracle. There is no reference to this visit in other passages of the Bible. The Canaanite woman came crying out, "Lord, Son of David, have mercy on me! My daughter is suffering terribly from demon-possession."

Voice 2

A keen look at the incident shows that three things were against her. Firstly, she was not a Jew. Secondly, her daughter was possessed by an evil spirit. Thirdly, she was crying aloud. People would have certainly thought very low of her for these reasons.

Voice 1

She addresses Jesus as "Lord" and "Son of David", thereby humbling herself and exalting the power of Jesus as "Lord" and "King." Traditionally, this act of hers is seen to be revealing her faith. At the same time, it points to her situation of powerlessness and despair. Initially, Jesus did not utter a word. His disciples too urged him:" Send her away, for she keeps crying out after us ." Only after this, Jesus replies to her. He refuses to acknowledge her request saying: "I was sent only to the lost sheep of Israel." Jesus rejects her ethnic background.

Voice 2

But the woman persisted with her request. She knelt before him and pleaded, "Lord, help me". Addressing him as "Lord", she tried to overcome the ethnic difference. Even though she addressed him as "Lord", it was not just an imploring voice, but a voice of protest too.

Voice 1

Her mode of addressing Jesus as Lord and King is traditionally interpreted as an act of faith. This is cited as an example for doing ministry among the gentiles. The way she knelt down and humbled herself is seen as a sign of self sacrifice. The response of Jesus is interpreted as an act of testing her faith. Jesus told her, "It is not right to take the children's bread and toss it to the dogs" (Matthew 15:26).

Voice 2

Yes, Lord", she said, "but even the dogs eat the crumbs that fall from their master's table." Though she addressed Jesus as Lord and allowed him to call her a dog, she opposed him and differed from him. She says: "Yes, Lord, but …"

Voice 1

It is always said that Jesus acknowledged her perseverance. He told her, "Woman, you have great faith! Your request is granted". Perhaps, that is why the Church of South India has titled the topic for today's meditation as "Faith and Culture– A Beneficial Change.".

Voice 2

The good thing about the episode is that she achieved what she wanted. Her daughter got healed. However, there are a few issues in the story.

Firstly, Jesus spoke to her harshly. Moreover, he called her a dog and made her realize her marginalized existence. So, the woman's culture was not respected.

Secondly, the woman could recognize him only as "Lord" and "King" by her mode of address. The identity of a "suffering servant" was not to be found here.

Thirdly, this story had also been used against the Jews. Since Jesus healed her daughter even when she happened to be powerless, her "faith" is attributed to be superior to that of the Jews.

At the same time, the story is also used to justify colonialism. The woman acted very humbly. Colonialism has taught us that this is "faith".

Voice 1

The Church has problems in looking at its history. We feel the missionaries have helped us to raise our standard of living, to learn new skills and to give new meaning to life. However, we are not able to see how the oppressive values of the colonial culture go along with the oppressive values in our own culture. The Christian communities too are divided on the basis of caste. Globalization has put people against people and has deepened the rift between rich and poor.

Voice 2

The feminist liberation theology has enabled us to see the story in a new light. This is the only story in which a person, seeking healing by Jesus, is voicing her protest to him. Though Jesus replied to her negatively initially, he fulfilled her wish ultimately.

In the banquet of Jesus, the oppressed, sinners, tax collectors, lepers and gentiles were called to participate. God's discretion of "sofia" (Wisdom) gathers people together. The Lord or King as a power centre condemns others and rejects them. But the discretion of "sofia" is compassionate and loving.

If one looks at the story from the perspective of "sofia" (Wisdom), one cannot justify its use against the Jews. For, even the Jews had faith in the spirit of discretion. When Matthew wrote the gospel, he had changed his earlier position of "converting the Jews first."

When we look at history from this backdrop, we come to face it that there is a connection between religious conversion and colonialism. At the same time, we cannot justify a colonial culture that condemns and marginalizes others. We must turn towards the spirit of liberation that is against the colonial culture. Above all, we should turn to the spirit of healing which encouraged the woman. She had the will and she wanted her daughter to live.

Amen.

* * * *

16. MALE AND FEMALE –
STRUCTURAL SINS AND REPENTANCE
Mark 10:17-31, Genesis 1:26-31

The topic this Sunday is "Forgiveness of Sins". At the same time, we are also commemorating International Working Women's Day, March 8th. It may therefore be helpful to reflect on the sinful structures of society, which endorse violence against women, keep the poor in subjugation and disempower the mass of the toiling people, Dalits, Adivasis, peasants and unorganized workers. What is the scope for repentance from such sinful structures? When John the Baptist raised his voice, he preached repentance. When Jesus healed people, he asked them to start a new life. Are we willing to listen to this call for repentance and change our lives or are we getting paralysed by the structures of injustice? Are we able to recall the wholeness of God's good creation and to regain the vision of God's reign, in which this wholeness will be recovered?

One of the key texts, which speaks about the difficulty to leave behind sinful structures, is the story of the rich young man who asks Jesus what he must do to inherit eternal life (Mk.10:17-31). It is important to read this text not just as the story of an individual, but to understand that it is the crisis of the Jesus community, which is expressed here. The disciples are fighting among each other who is the greatest. They are rebuking the children which are brought to Jesus, but Jesus admits them and blesses them. When the rich young man calls upon Jesus as a "good teacher", Jesus rebukes him not to call him "good", because nobody is good than God alone. He repeats the commandments: Do not kill. Do not commit adultery. Do not steal. Do not bear false witness. Do not cheat. Honour your father and mother. The young man says he has followed them all. Jesus looks at him and loves him. He then asks him to sell what he has and give it to the poor and to follow him. At that saying his countenance falls and he goes away sorrowfully for he had great possessions.

Jesus then immediately applies this experience to the ongoing discussion about the Jesus community. "How hard it will be for those who have riches to enter the Kigdom of God. It is easier for a camel to go through the eye of a needle than for a rich man to enter the Kingdom of God". The disciples immediately understand the predicament and ask: "Then who can be saved?" Jesus replies: "With man it is impossible, but not with God". In today's day and age of the prosperity gospel, this is often taken as some sort of gracious head trick of God: Shrinking the camel to save the rich man. But of course what Jesus told the rich young man was to sell the riches and give them to the poor - distribution of what has been acquired through exploitation. It is this which is difficult to achieve. Peter then says: "We have left everything behind and followed you". Jesus replies: "There is no one who has left house or brothers or sisters or mother or father or children or lands, for my sake and for the gospel, who will not receive a hundred fold now in this time, houses and brothers and sisters and mothers and children and lands, with persecutions, and in the age to come eternal life. But many that are the first will be last".

The new community will be based on sharing and it will not be ruled by fathers. It is a community without patriarchy in which equals will serve one another. This is indeed difficult to achieve. Dismantling the attachment to wealth and the attachment to power and hierarchy, needs to go together with dismantling patriarchy.

How do we do this? I think we have to first of all acknowledge that patriarchy itself is sin. We have to understand that the way the story of the Fall in Gen.3 is told, is itself depicting the fall into patriarchy. It justifies women's subordination in a patriarchal society. However, this subordination of women is not inherent in God's good creation, nor is it envisaged in the new community, which Jesus was trying to create and which prefigures the new relationships in God's reign. We need to gain more clarity about this. We have to stop telling Gen.3 like a marriage drama between Mr.Adam and Mrs.Eve, in which the woman, beguiled by the snake, tempts her husband, who without being suspicious listens to her and falls into a mortal trap. Within this logic, we have to point out that not eating from the tree was told to Mr., while Mrs. was not yet in the picture. In this version, the woman is depicted as the origin of sin and the children in Sunday class are sent home with the memory verse: "The wage of sin is death". Thus, women, the givers of Life, are depicted as the source of sin, evil and death. This is a technique of denigration, which has been called "reversal". As we know, this distorted reading of Gen.3 has been carried over into texts of Paul and the pastoral letters, which justify women's subordination. We cannot go on preaching on these texts as if nothing is the matter. On the other hand it is important to understand that the text of Gen.1:26-31, which we have kept as a reading for this service, uses the term "Adam" as a generic term, "human being", made from adamah, Mother Earth. Here it is said from the outset: male and female God created them, both in God's image. The question of patriarchal subordination does not arise here. Gen.1 belongs to the priestly source, compiled in the time of the Babylonian Exile, while Gen.2 and 3 belong to the Jahvist source which belongs to the 8th century when kingship and patriarchy were in full power. But even in this older source, the term Adam is used as a generic term, "the earth creature", made from Earth, Adamah. Differentiation into male and female happens only from chapter 3:18 onwards, and even here the aim is equality and companionship: Flesh, of my flesh, bone of my bone, not subordination. The question who was first is not of importance here, because first was the Earth and all the other creatures. The term "Helper", which is used here, does not express subordination either. It can be used among equals, it can also be used for the powerful, like in Psalm 121: "I lift up my eyes to the hills: From hence does my help come? My help comes from the Lord who made heaven and earth". The text in Gen.1:26-31 not only envisages equality between women and men but even gives dominion over other creatures to both of them. The Hebrew word which is used here, is a very strong term usually used for despotic rule. This use of language is not unproblematic. Eco-theologians have pointed out that christianized Europe has been insensitive to ecology and has betrayed the relationship between Adam and Adamah, human beings and the earth.

This betrayal of the relationship between human beings and the Earth today takes forms of enormous destructiveness all over the globe. During the recent visit of George Bush to Delhi, Mumbai and Hyderabad, a new nuclear treaty has been signed, which has most dangerous implications for expansion of nuclear energy production and proliferation of nuclear weapons. Such development can devastate the earth beyond human imagination.

It is highly absurd that the country, which terrorises the world with its superior weaponry, does all this in the name of "democracy" and also considers itself as a champion of women's liberation. It is at this point that we need to return to the story of the rich young man and its significance for the Jesus community. The prosperity Gospel of George Bush cannot be redeemed by a hat trick of shrinking the camel. It leads to nuclear disaster as logical consequence. But the masses of the poor in Latin America have once again risen up and said no to this kind of exploitative hegemony. Chile has elected a socialist woman Michelle Bachelet as a President and Bolivia has elected Evo Morales, a representative of the indigenous communities.

These are signs of the times which give hope and which connect us with the struggles of International Women's Day. But our homework of building the new communities, we have to do at home, in our own families and our own institutions. We have to wake up to the day to day violence in our own environment, where women are raped and beaten, where children are abused and do not dare to speak out. Jesus called the women and children into his presence. He quarreled with his disciples when they wanted to keep things under control. He calls us to repentance and new community. This is his way of redeeming the sin of patriarchy. Are we listening?

(March 12, 2006)

* * * *

17. ELIMINATING A WITNESS

Luke 24:13-35

Jesus the risen one reveals himself to two of the disciples of the wider circle around him, on the way to the village of Emmaus. We are all familiar with this. "Stay with us, for it is towards evening and the day is now far spent". This text is often used as an evening prayer. It has a reassuring mood.

However, let us look at it afresh, in the sharp morning light of the resurrection. It is in many ways a disturbing text. It raises questions about our perceptions of his presence. Especially, the text contrasts the experiences of male disciples with those of female disciples. At the same time, the text does not also value fully the Easter witness of the women.

As we have seen in the end of chapter 23, the women who had come with Jesus from Galilee followed Joseph of Arimathia when he took the body for burial. The women observed how the body was laid and then went to prepare ointment and spices. Due to this practical activity of looking after the body they were present at the empty grave and met the angels. In the other gospels, they also meet Jesus, or at least it is mentioned that Mary of Magdala was the first witness to the resurrection, the first person Jesus spoke to after he took on a new Body. This is left out in Luke. Nevertheless we are told that the women who had come with him from Galilee as a group told "to the eleven and the rest" that Jesus was risen. We are also told that this was dismissed as idle talk. We find explicitly mention of Mary of Magdala, Joanna, Mary the mother of Jesus and the other women. This is thus not an isolated statement of one or two witnesses. It is the women as a group who told the male disciples that they had met the angels and that those had conveyed that he had risen on the third day, as Jesus himself had earlier announced. We all know that women had to face restrictions in being accepted as witnesses in a Jewish court. However, this situation goes far beyond that. The women as a group hold the view that Jesus is risen and they quote Jesus' own announcement of his resurrection. Nevertheless this is dismissed as idle talk.

From this event the text goes over to the story of the two disciples on their way to Emmaus. However, some of the sources have taken trouble to shove in a verse which states that Peter ran to the tomb, stooped and looked and saw the folded clothes and went home wondering what had happened. Other sources leave this verse out as it seems to be a later addition.

However this may be, we hear next that two male disciples of the wider circle around Jesus were walking on their way to the village of Emmaus. Jesus drew near and he went with them without them recognising him. When he asks about their conversation, the disciple called Cleopas asks him: "Are you the only one who does not know what has happened these days in Jerusalem?" Then they narrate his own story to him. They speak of him as a mighty prophet crucified by the chief priests and rulers. They also tell that they had hoped that he would redeem Israel. Further, they mention the women who went to the tomb, saw the grave empty, met the angel and witnessed that Jesus was alive. They also say that "some of us", i.e. the men, went to see the grave empty but did not see the Lord.

Obviously, despite all this evidence, they still cannot see, "their eyes are held", it is said. They have a severe mental block to believe what they see despite Jesus' own earlier announcement that he would rise. This mental block provokes considerable anger in Jesus. The risen one scolds them in no uncertain terms. In v.25 we hear that Jesus calls the male disciples "Foolish men and slow of heart to believe all that the prophets have spoken". There he goes on to explain to them about Moses and the prophets. Despite all of this, the scolding and the teaching, the male disciples are so benighted that they still do not understand what is going on. It is hard to believe how far this stubbornness goes.

They continue on their way and near Emmaus Jesus appears to be going further. They restrain him and invite him: "Stay with us, for it is towards evening and the day is now far spent". It is they who extend an invitation, apparently protecting him from the night. But in reality, it is they who need him to bring light into the darkness of their blocked minds. It is they who are in the dark. As long as they do not understand about the resurrection, despite so much evidence, they are without courage and without a direction.

It is therefore a logical conclusion that it is he who blesses the bread, breaks it and gives it to them. It is he who hosts and feeds them. It is through this physical, material sign of the eucharist that their eyes are opened. But as they recognise him through this sign, he vanishes.

Only then, in retrospect, they remember how their hearts burnt while he spoke to them on the road and explained the scripture. They hurriedly go to Jerusalem and find the eleven disciples. Those now say (v.34) that the Lord has risen indeed and appeared to Simon. This is a strange statement because the actual event of Jesus' appearing to Simon is nowhere narrated, not even if we presume that v.12 which some of the sources have added, is authentic. The two disciples from Emmaus now tell how they have met Jesus on the road and he talked to them and how they recognised him only in the breaking of the bread.

There are three things which are noteworthy in this narrative of Luke:

1. One aspect is the strong contradiction between male and female disciples. The words of the risen one are particularly harsh. Like in the other gospels, the male disciples cut a poor picture in times of crisis. They are found napping in Gethsemane. One of them cuts off the ear of the slave of the high priest when the soldiers come and Peter denies Jesus three times after the arrest. However, in Luke the Emmaus story works out the contrast with more emphasis: Over three verses (22-24) we hear how the women amazed the disciples by their witness that the tomb was empty and that the angels had told that he was alive. Some of the male disciples went and found the tomb as the women had said but they could not see. For this, the response of the risen one is harsh and impatient. He calls them fools and slow of heart to believe all that the prophets have spoken. This includes obviously, also what the women have spoken.

2.   Despite the emphasis on the contradiction between female and male disciples, Luke   is the only evangelist who does not recognise Mary of Magdala as the first witness to the resurrection. In Mark (16:9-11) we   find the very sober and matter of fact statement that Jesus first appeared to Mary of Magdala from whom he had cast out seven demons. Matthew continues the narrative of the angel with the appearance of Jesus to Mary of Magdala and the other Mary (Mt.28:1-11) and John has an expanded version where Mary of Magdala thinks he was the gardener. Only Luke has suppressed the appearance of Jesus to Mary of Magdala and maintains instead that Jesus appeared to Simon (Lk.24:34) and other male disciples.   This is incongruent even if one takes v.12 into account which mentions Simon going to the grave, but only says that he found it empty but did not see Jesus. Luke therefore is an important link in the chain of narratives where women have been made to disappear from the records on the revelation of the risen one.

3. It is difficult to find a clear explanation how in Luke Mary of Magdala was eliminated as the first witness to the resurrection. We know from feminist research that in the early church there was a power struggle about leadership in which there was a conflict between Mary of Magdala and Simon Peter. But why did Luke choose to eliminate Mary's most crucial experience?

One explanation may be that the emphasis in Luke is on Jerusalem. The encounter in chapter 24 is in Emmaus which as we know from other sources like Flavius Josephus was a Roman Garrison town.   Luke wrote after the destruction of Jerusalem. He wrote in a situation of utmost devastation and hopelessness. Yet he tried to uphold the perspective that Jesus had come to redeem Israel (v.21). The disciples rush back to Jerusalem to meet the eleven. In Luke, the scene of the revelation of the risen one is in Jerusalem while in the other Gospels Jesus goes ahead of them to Galilee. In Luke even the broiled fish which one would expect to belong to the lake of Galilee is consumed in Jerusalem (v.43). He rises up to heaven in Bethany, not in Galilee. The disciples return to the temple to praise God. The women, on the contrary, clearly belong to Galilee. Mary belongs to Migdal on the lake. Luke seems to try to uphold a Messianic anti-colonial statement against the victorious Roman empire. This appears to be honourable: Upholding Jerusalem and the temple in the face of a victorious colonial power which has destroyed the city. For this political assertion he needs Peter as the leader of the church. For this he sacrifices Mary of Magdala. He makes her invisible as the first witness of the resurrection.

There are many examples where women are silenced in order to uphold the "correct" ideology. If a leftist woman is beaten by her husband, she will be told not to raise family matters but to speak about the landlord. If a dalit woman criticises patriarchal behaviour in a dalit man, she will be asked: Are you a dalit? If women raise their voice in the church they are told not to disturb peace. It is necessary to remember the risen one scolding the men as foolish and slow of heart. It is good to remember that it is women who proclaim resurrection and uprising.

(December 11, 1997)

* * * *

IV. WISDOM AND FOLLY

18. THE FOLLY OF THE CROSS
I Corinthians 1:18-25; Luke 23:26-33

The above texts speak of the folly of the cross and of the wisdom of this world. I will first comment on the text in the first letter to the Corinthians and will then connect this with the concrete scene which is specific to the Gospel of Luke. This is known as Jesus' lamentation over the women of Jerusalem and in the Catholic tradition it is the eighth station of the cross. I will then try to raise the question what the texts means in today's context.

The text in first Corinthians is probably the older of the two. It is written in a problematic situation. Corinth in those times was an important harbor city, a cosmopolitan place, something like Bombay. The members of this Church were to a large extent from the harbor proletariat of Corinth. As we hear in v.26: "according to worldly standards, not many were powerful, and not many were of noble birth". But of course there were also the educated slaves who were clerks in the administration, there were people who knew how to do business and there were those who spoke in tongues, there were the philosophers and also the Gnostics, those who tried to tread the path of wisdom. As a result, the Christians whom Paul had converted, were divided among each other. A woman called Chloe, a leader of the harbor workers, had complained about this (v.11).

Against all these divisions, Paul upholds the foolishness of the Cross. He starts off by saying (v.18)": "The word of the cross is folly to those who are perishing but to us who are being saved it is the power of God". This thought is reversed in v.25 where Paul speaks of the foolishness of God. The foolishness of God is wiser than men, and the weakness of God is stronger than men. There is no role for the wise men, the scribes, the debates.

This means, there was no role for the theologians, the philosophers, the experts or, on the other hand, the evangelicals the fundamentalists. Everything is questioned by the folly of the cross.

The divisions in Corinth have to do with mutual mistrust. Each faction wants to control and to push their point. Each does not want the others to come up. The theologians and philosophers want to pursue their theories and want to control the illiterates by their monopoly on expertise and education. The inspired believers try to speak in tongues and may try to speak in a louder voice than the others. They may try to make their point by noise and force of numbers. But Paul cuts through the whole controversy by upholding the folly of the cross. The Jews want signs, and the Greek seek wisdom (v.22). But Christ crucified is a stumbling block to the Jews and a folly to the Gentiles (v.23) Christ crucified is the power of God and the wisdom of God.

This is indeed quite mad because the cross is an instrument of torture. It is a symbol of death and defeat. This means that success is not a yardstick to measure truth. This is of course something which we have learned in the women's movement and in the methodology of 'subaltern studies'. Making the underside of history visible means to recover the dimension of the resurrection for our defeats.

I now turn to Jesus' lamentation over the women of Jerusalem. Jesus is on his way to crucifixion. He has been tortured and ridiculed and has stumbled several times. They have caught a man Simon of Kyrene to bear the cross for him and the crowds are with him. The women are beating their breasts and wailing. These are not the crowds who had demanded of Pilate to crucify Jesus and to release Barabas.   These are people who are with Jesus and who cry over his impending death.

But Jesus turns to them and says: "Daughters of Jerusalem, do not weep for me, but weep for yourself and your children" (v.20). For behold, the days are coming when they will say: "Blessed are the barren and the wombs that never bore and the breasts that, never gave suck"!

This is an image of utter despair and destruction. It is specific to Luke who refers to the destruction of Jerusalem several times. This image of barrenness is followed up by another image which amounts to suicide: Let the mountains fall on us. If we allow those who live a life of truthfulness to die like cattle, and allow the criminals who promote violence to live, then we commit a collective suicide. Jesus compels people to see what happens to themselves in this process. He compels them to think and recognize their own situation. This does not mean a futuristic expectation of destruction but a thinking process which anticipates and leads into action. The wisdom of this world leads to more violence and to collective suicide. Yet the absurd truth is that this destruction and defeat is not the last word. Those who are defeated share in the resurrection. Those who are in the clutches of the wisdom of this world, of easy success, commit a collective suicide and victimize others.

What does all this mean in today's situation? We are living at a moment in history where the wisdom of this world is taking over in unprecedented ways. The gospel of globalization and unlimited economic growth, the gospel of mammon and the World Bank, demands unconditional faith. Those of us who resist this brave new world appear as real fools who do not understand the signs of the times. We are living at a moment in history where the ideologues, the experts, the promoters of science and technology, have taken over. The Gospel of this type of economic success is also promoted by the evangelicals and fundamentalists. Many of the main stream churches have also jumped on this band wagon. We know today that structural adjustment is a form of collective suicide. The tragedy is that those who resist, are murdered like Shankar Guha Niyogi and the many martyrs of the Chattisgarh Mukti Morcha.

How do we resist the wisdom of this world and how do we hold on in to the foolishness of the cross? This is of course a very difficult question and we need to ponder it in depth. I can think of some examples.

1. In school our children are constantly taught the survival of the fittest. They are taught to compete for marks at all costs. But they do not allow themselves to be pitted against each other. They try to be supportive of the weak and to share their knowledge. We can encourage them to learn from those who are illiterate but who have the wisdom of suffering and who know that life is only possible in mutual support.

2. Corruption has taken on unprecedented proportion. This not only extracts money from the poor, it also leads to violence and rowdyism. Resisting this tendency is very tedious. But if we surrender to the terror of mammon, we destroy life at its root. Jesus encourages us to see what happens to ourselves in this process.

3. We may have to learn to dissent and to take decisions which require a risk. This may be difficult because we are all the time expected to adjust. Jesus himself did not conform to the society, the family or to the rules of his religion. He disobeyed, he provoked, he was a misfit and utter failure. He calls us to radical discipleship. Unto death, unto resurrection, unto uprising.

(October 1993)

* * * *

19. WORDS AND DEEDS
James 3

The letter of James has two main concerns, which have created controversy. One concern is with the insistence that faith without works is dead (2:14-17). This seems to go against the central conviction of Paul and the reformation, that justifications springs from faith alone. James insists that faith without deeds is irrelevant. The second central concern of this letter is with the poor. The letter warns very thoroughly not to give any privilege to the rich, because they are exploiters. God, on the contrary, has chosen the poor to be rich in faith and heirs of the kingdom (25). It is on the background of these two basic insights that the third chapter of the letter has to be read.

Chapter three elaborates on the dangers of faith without deeds, consisting of mere talking. The initial verses 1-6 can be read as a special warning to teachers and pastors. V.1 says explicitly. Let not many of you become teachers, because "we who teach shall be judged with greater strictness". The author clearly includes himself in this judgement. He then goes on to say: "We all make mistakes and if anybody makes no mistakes in what he says, he is a perfect man, able to bridle the whole body also".

He compares the role of the tongue with the bit in a horse's mouth by which the horse is bridled. He also compares the tongue with a small rudder which steers a big ship. But unlike the bit and the rudder, the tongue itself is out of control. He calls it" a little member which boasts of great things" and then adds. "How great a forest is set ablaze by a small fire". While the bit and the rudder are seen as beneficial, so they control the power of the horse and master the forces of nature like storm and waves, the tongue itself is seen as an instrument of destruction. Words have power, they can build and they can destroy. The tongue "boasts", it creates greatness where there is none and it denigrates, curses, destroys, often in the same breath.

The next passage, v.6-12, elaborates on the destructive power of the tongue. V.6 gives a very devastating judgement: "The tongue is a fire. It is an unrighteous world among our members, staining the whole body". The next sentence is even more extreme. "It sets on fire the cycle of nature and is set on fire by hell". Nature itself can be destructive, as different species feed on each other. But nature is also prolific; it brings forth life all the time. So, there is a balance in nature, if nature is left to itself.

The author points out that humankind is capable to tame every kind of beast, bird, reptile or sea creature. Then he goes to say: "But no human being can tame the tongue, - a restless evil, full of deadly poison".

The reason he gives is interesting: With the tongue we bless the Lord and Father, but we curse humans who are made in the likeness of God. From the same mouth come blessing and cursing.

This ought not to be so. Brackish water and sweet water cannot pour forth from the same spring. A fig tree cannot yield olives, a grapevine cannot yield figs. Salt water cannot yield fresh water...

The final five verses of the chapter show the alternative to this destructive behaviour. "Who is wise and understanding among you? By his good life let him show his works on the meekness of wisdom". Wisdom is expressed in living a good life. It is expressed in our lifestyle, in our deeds, in our human relations. The enemy of this wisdom is bitter jealousy and selfish ambition.

Ambition and selfishness lead to a wisdom which is devilish and unspiritual. It leads to competition, to disorder and vile practices. The chapter closes with upholding this true wisdom. Wisdom from above is pure, peaceable, gentle, open to reason, full of mercy and good fruits, without uncertainty and insincerity. The destructive behaviour comes out of uncertainty and insincerity. This indeed needs to be overcome. To overcome uncertainty and insincerity, faith is essential, a faith lived in deeds. The final verse ends the chapter with a promise. The harvest of righteous-ness is sown in peace by those who make peace. In contrast to the first two parts of the chapter, which highlight the destructiveness of words, the constructive aspect of right living is now affirmed. This is very encouraging. The next two chapters go into the reasons of war and discord among people. They elaborate on the topic of greed, ambition and slander. The killing of the righteous is the result. God judges but he is also compassionate.

Sticking to the message of chapter three of James' letter, there are different ways in which this can be read. We can read it in the context of ordinary politics in church congregations and institutions. I think it is not at all difficult to recognize the situation. Ambition, slander, wielding of power are going on in many places. This is rooted not only in misuse of power, competition and greed; it is also rooted in insecurity and lack of faith. This leads to destruction of human relations and many court cases. The writer of the letter poses a challenge to build peace through right living. This is very encouraging.

I think there is also a second way of reading this chapter in today's context. It takes on a new meaning in the era of globalisation with its rising fundamentalism and postmodernism. The scathing critique of the "tongue" can be read as a critique of ideology. We are warned to have a reality check: Does what we say really correspond to what we do? The reality check is with respect to the cycle of nature. Are we setting it on fire? Are we destroying the forests, the water table? Are we causing global warming?

It is necessary to understand that words are not innocent. If the American President speaks of "democracy" and unleashes brutal wars on Afghanistan and Iraq, he blesses God and curses human beings, he kills and maims them. This happened in the course of a "war on terrorism", but terrorism has been first of all nurtured by the same forces who now say they fight against it.

In our own country we constantly experience a situation where an enemy is created and people are killed and denigrated in the name of religion. Most often this happens to Muslims. But it also leads to a situation where the victims can only think of themselves as victims and lose their capacity to gain freedom and build peace.

The crucial question is how to reconstruct society in the spirit of wisdom and peace. How can we do this in real life? I am writing this while attending a whole series of trade union meetings of workers in the informal sector. The problem in this sector is that , it is divided by political parties and their ideologies. Nobody means what they say, its all a power game. But the genuine unions are rebuilding the human relations, are sowing the seeds of wisdom and peace, even while being under threat of their life. The bonded labourers of Red Hills in Chennai are under threat of being cut to pieces like in the movie Kajendran. The tongue becomes a raging fire that kills.

This is not a question of deconstructing and reconstructing our language. It is a matter of reinventing our lifestyle together with the poor and in support of the forces of nature. Without learning this wisdom, there can't be peace.

(October 6, 2004)

* * * *

20. THE CALL OF WISDOM

Matthew 6:24-34; Isaiah 65:17-25; Proverbs 8:22-36

The Gospel text (Matt.6:25-34) comes towards the later part of the Sermon of the Mount. Do not be anxious. It needs to be read together with v.24: No one can serve two masters; you cannot serve God and Mammon. Significantly, v.24 has been cut off in the lectionary of the church. So we are left only with the admonition not to be anxious about what we eat, what we drink, what we clothe ourselves with.

It feels strange to read this text after the tsunami which had hit the Asian coastlines on December 26th, 2004. "Which of you by being anxious can add one cubit to the span of his life?" This sounds ironic. It sounds like: Anyway, there is no escape.

But this is not what this text is trying to tell us. It tries to tell us that the nations are running after power and money in the name of these worries of: What shall we eat, what shall we drink, what shall we wear? We are told: Seek you first the kingdom of God and its righteousness, and all these things shall be yours as well. What does this mean?

How to envisage the promised salvation? If we look at the prophetic text (Is.65:17-25) it is a picture of the New Jerusalem. This is a text which belongs to the post-exilic period of reconstruction after the Babylonian exile (around 530 BC). People have come back to Jerusalem. However, the people to whom it is addressed are still living in

poverty and utmost political insecurity.   The interesting
aspect in this chapter is that it does not aim at any one
definite event which will bring salvation. It does not
promise the reconstruction of the temple or the annihilation
of enemies.   It speaks of rejoicing and gladness. No more
weeping, no cries of distress. No dying infants. They shall
not labour in vain. Women shall not bear children for
calamity. They shall build houses and inhabit them. They
shall plant vineyards and eat their fruit. The wolf and the
lamb shall feed together, the lion shall eat straw like the
ox; dust shall be the serpents' food. "They shall not hurt or
destroy in all my holy mountain", says the Lord. This is
the vision of the kingdom for which Jesus tells his disciples
to strive. A peace not built on annihilation of others or on
deterrence.

The text promises food, shelter, security and a long life.
Yet, we are told in the Sermon of the Mount, not to strive
for food, shelter, security and a long life. It does not seem
to make sense. The point of course is that this vision of
peace is rooted in the close relationship with God, while
the security against which Jesus warns has to do with the
striving for money. Striving for money brings inequality,
exploitation and strife, it does not allow peace.

But what about the tsunami? Hasn't God let the people
down? Those who called on him at the shrine of our Lady
of Good Health in Velankanni? The people in the fishing
villages, the children playing on the beach, born for
calamity?

I do not think I have clear answers to these questions.
But it strikes me that there is a third text given from the
chapter 8 of the book of Proverbs, vs.22-31. I think it is

necessary to extend the text up to v.36. This text speaks about wisdom. Wisdom herself speaks in this text. She speaks like a person. Who is she?

We are not speaking of wisdom in this personal quality in the church very often. The commentaries acknowledge that wisdom as a feminine figure has connections with the goddesses of ancient Egypt and Babylon. In the book of Proverbs, we mostly hear of wisdom in the sense of sayings or teachings. However, in the first chapter of the book, the direction is given in Prov.1:10-19. These verses warn of people who are willing to shed blood for gain. "For in vain is a net spread in the sight of any bird; but these men lie in wait of their own blood, they set an ambush for their own lives. Such are the ways of all who get gain by violence; it takes away the life of its possessors", (Prov.1:17-19).

In the following verses wisdom is introduced as a person who cries aloud in the street, raises her voice in the market place on top of the walls and in the entrance of the city gates. But here she is also full of bitterness for not being listened to and threatens with destruction. In chapter 8, this direct speech of wisdom is taken up again. She cries out from the streets, from the heights besides the ways. She calls people to learn prudence (8:4). From her mouth comes truth and righteousness, there is nothing crooked in her words. She hates pride and arrogance. Those who rule justly, do this through her. She gives riches and honour and enduring wealth and prosperity, which is better than the finest gold and silver. She walks in the way of righteousness and the path of justice.

In the second half of chapter 8 she tries to explain where she came from. She says that God created her at the beginning of his work, the first of his acts of old (8:22). She is present during the whole act of creation like a master workman. "When he made the firm skies above, the fountains of the deep, when he assigned the sea its limit that the waters might not transgress his command, when he marked out the foundations of the earth, I was there as a master workman, and I was a daily delight, rejoicing before him always, rejoicing in his inhabited world and delighting in the sons of men".

In the end of the chapter, she exhorts people to listen to her ways. "For he who finds me finds life and obtains favour from God, but he who misses me, injures himself; all who hate me love death" (8:35-36).

Her message is that nature cannot be trapped and taken advantage of, that humans cannot be subjugated and exploited. The spirit of this chapter connects directly with the gospel text of Matt.6: You cannot serve God and Mammon. Only if you leave behind the pursuit of riches, if you strive for a way of living where everybody can dwell in peace and enjoy the fruit of their labour, you will find life. Otherwise, you will end up loving death.

Does this make sense in this situation where the wrath of nature has stricken and the sea has annihilated lakhs of lives? In many places the living envy the dead. Innumerable children have died. But there are incidents which make us think. We hear that few animals have died in the tsunami, because they have an instinct knowledge when disaster strikes. Humans have to use their brains and power of discernment and become panicky easily. There were reports in the newspapers about a ten years old school girl from England, Tilly, who was on a holiday in Thailand and recognized the symptoms of the tsunami in time, because she remembered what she had been taught in school. She mustered courage and convinced others. She saved many lives by raising a warning on the beach. She had more wisdom than the embassies who did not contact the home ministry. But of course this is only a stray incident.

It has been recognized in the meantime that one of the key factors in the enormous loss of life is different. We have done violence to our coast since decades. Wherever there was tree cover and mangrove forest, people have been protected. The very name of the mangrove in some places is 'kadal aatri', the pacifier of the sea. The coastline has been destroyed by huge tourism enterprises, prawn farms, and poisonous industries, including even nuclear plants. The coastal regulation zone has been violated right and left. The law has been diluted by amendments. The political parties are vying with each other to push ahead the Sethu Samuthiram project, dredging a deep canal between India and Sri Lanka. This will destroy coral reefs, marine life, fisheries. It will deepen the conflict with the fishermen.

All this happens in the pursuit of more money. It has been happening all along. It is not that we don't know it. Some of us are actively resisting it in various struggles of people's movements. But the trend is in the opposite direction. The most powerful nation in the world preaches the gospel of money as God's blessing and expands its military reach in the name of disaster relief and scientific expertise. It also pours money into conversions to spread the gospel of mammon more effectively and to control water and oil all over the world. Many Christians sing Halleluja to all this.

It is good to remember wisdom in this situation. Wisdom shouting for social justice on the streets, wisdom delighting in the beauty of God's creation since the dawn of life and calling us to leave our foolish ways and to choose life!   Amen.

(January 23, 2005)

* * * *

21. THE SPIRIT AS COUNSELLOR

John 16

Chapter 15 and 16 of the gospel of John are in a way a different version of the same message which has been given in the farewell addresses in chapter 13:31 till 14:31. All these chapters deal with the coming of the Spirit.

The crucial messages have been there in 14:15-17 and in 15:26. In chapter 16 Jesus spells out the full meaning of his going away and of the coming of the counsellor in his stead.

So in a way chapter 16 is about the meaning of separation, coming of age, taking responsibility, suffering in the process and being comforted.

The context in which the separation is set is a serious one. Jesus fore-spells persecution and death for the disciples: The hour is coming when whoever kills you will think he is offering service to God. This, obviously is ground for anxiety. There will be fear in the face of persecution and death.

1. However, the first statement which Jesus makes counters this fear (v.7).

It is to your advantage that I go away for if I do not go away, the Counsellor will not come to you. But if I go, I will send him to you.

This is the first important point. Without Jesus' going, the counsellor will not be sent. Separation is necessary without separation, no new life.

2.   The second important point is about what the counsellor will do. The counsellor is specified as *"the spirit of truth"*. As such the image of the councellor comes very close to two key concepts in the Old Testament: *chesed* faithfulness and *emeth*, truth.

The counsellor, says v.8, will convince the world concerning sin, righteousness and judgement.

*   "Sin because they do not believe in me". Believing in him means: abiding in love, abiding in friendship, not in servitude. It also means handing over to the disciples.

*   Concerning righteousness: "because I go to the father and you will see me no more". This has to do with taking responsibility, coming of age. As long as Jesus is present, the disciples have relied that Jesus will tell them what is right and wrong. Now that he goes to the father and they see him no more, the disciples themselves have to decide what is right or wrong. Coming of age, taking responsibility and righteousness are going together.

The councellor also brings judgement because the ruler of this world is judged. The ruler of this world - satan - by another name *diabolos* - the one who divides, confuses, turns people against each other, divide and rule.

As we have seen above, the spirit of truth is also the spirit of love and friendship. The spirit of satan is the spirit of servitude and divisiveness. This spirit is judged.

To sum up: Jesus describes the situation which leads to his death and resurrection. Sin describes the breakdown of faith and love, which leads to betrayal and death.

However, it is this going away of Jesus, his death, which reveals a righteousness which is not of this world. This, in turn, reveals that the ruler of this world is judged.

3. The third important part of this text deals more directly with death and resurrection v.16. "A little while and you will see me no more. Again a little while and you will see me". This appears totally incomprehensible in a situation where the events of the cross and resurrection cannot yet be imagined. Jesus therefore uses the image of childbirth to make his point:

> v.21 "When a woman is in travail she has sorrow, because her hour has come; but when she is delivered of the child, she no longer remembers the anguish, for joy that a child is born into the world".

Resurrection cannot be had without death and separation. The chapter closes with the vision that everyone will be scattered. But it finally closes with a note of comfort: "Be of good cheer. I have overcome the world".

I would now like to reflect on this text in the context of today's situation, our own as well as the world at large.

1. Separation, coming of age, taking responsibility are not topics which are easy to face. They are also faced differently by women and men. Decision making is something which is usually borne collectively and parents are expected to decide for the children, the elders for the younger members. Each person makes experiences from childhood where our own aspirations get rejected and thwarted. We feel weak and vulnerable and much of the time we are looking for support and council from people whom we perceive as more experienced and more powerful.

However, this insecurity is also at the root of leadership cult. The leader makes promises, people follow. If the goods are not delivered, there may be anger, violence, destruction.

2. Women are usually seen as less capable of decision making. As daughters, sisters, wives and mothers we are supposed to be decided upon. However, in reality women have to cope with separation more than men. The girl child knows she will be separated from her parental home. When a woman gives birth, she has to separate the child from her own body in a violent and painful process. Later again she will be separated from the children she has borne as the children start their own lives. When the girl child attains age, she is separated from her usual environment and subjected to new controls. All this is painful but she learns to deal with her pain and takes responsibility in a different way.

3. As the academic year comes to an end, the final year students have to separate from the life in the seminary. The big TTS family will no longer be there to guide them and in the diocese they may feel lonely amidst quarrels and court cases and power struggles which have little to do with social justice.

It may be good to remember in this situation the spirit of love and friendship of which Jesus speaks. Sin is to abandon this spirit. Righteousness is to discern the spirits even if we are lonely and without guidance. Judgement is the certainty that the ruler of this world is judged. The spirit of servitude and divisiveness is denied a future.

4. A similar situation prevails in society and in the world at large. With the onslaught of globalisation, we are

facing a situation in which the political fabric and the social structures disintegrate. The leadership either is corrupted as we see in the hawala case or the leaders get murdered as in the case of Shankar Guha Niyogi, this too connected with Hawala money.

If the corrupted leaders leave us, it will be to our good, this is evident. If the real leaders who have integrity also leave us, how can this be to our good?

It is hard to say. I have just been to Dalli Rajhara, the place of Niyogi and the CMM. The struggle there has not made any headway in terms of gains. The 4000 contract workers who had struggled 10 months when Niyogi was shot on 28th September 1991, have not been reinstated. But the movement still grows. New workers join the union and the peasant movement is expanding. People come in large numbers to the Shahid Hospital where they have to pay instead of using the free medical services offered by the management. They are sustained by the spirit of friendship and love, they have left the spirit of servitude behind. They have not heard of the death and resurrection of Jesus sayings. They have not heard of Jesus saying: In the world you have tribulations but be of good cheer, I have overcome the world. But they have learned to live in hope in the face of death. May we learn from them to live in uprising and resurrection.

(March 30, 1996)

* * * *

22. WHERE HAVE YOU LEFT MY LORD?

John 21

I would like to look into this chapter for what it makes visible and also for what it makes invisible in order to raise some questions about the church. Today's topic in the CSI is the Ministry, and most of the other texts given are about sacred vestments and ritual matters. The good thing about John 21 is that it is full of contradictions and uncertainties. This may help us to come to terms with our own contradictions and uncertainties.

John 21 deals with the situation after the resurrection. In this, it is directly related to chapter 20. In both the chapters, there is a lot of contradiction between who sees Jesus and how they perceive him:

Chapter 20 has the narrative of Mary of Magdala as the first witness to see the Risen Lord. She weeps outside the tomb and sees two angels sitting where Jesus was laid and the angels ask her: Woman, why are you weeping? The scene is reminiscent of the song of songs. It is set in a garden and Mary replied to the angels: "They have taken away my Lord and I do not know where they have laid him". It is a scene of separation, similar to Chapter 5 of the Song of Songs where the desolate woman faces the watchmen of Jerusalem as she searches for her beloved. When she sees Jesus, he asks her. "Woman, why are you weeping, whom do you seek?" She says: "If you have taken him away, tell me where you have laid him and I

will take him away". The recognition comes only when he
calls her by her name and she says: "Rabboni - my
teacher". Jesus says to her. "Do not hold me, for I have
not yet ascended to my father". The expectation is that
Mary would spontaneously embrace him. But she believes
without touching. It is on this ground that Mary goes to
the disciples and tells them that she has seen the Lord.

The other encounters of Jesus with his disciples in this
chapter are very different. We hear of the disciples
absconding and being full of fear on the evening of this
same day. Jesus greets them with peace and breathes the
Holy Spirit on them.

A similar scene is set eight days later, apparently in
order to take care of Thomas who had doubted as he was
not present on the evening of the first day and who insists
on touching the nail marks and the wound on the side.

Chapter 21 starts off right after these encounters and
the location is now shifted to the lake of Galilee. Jesus
encounters the disciples while they are fishing in the lake.
Jesus observes that the disciples have no fish. He
encourages them to throw the net out again and they make
such a big catch that they find it difficult to haul in the net.

On the shore, Jesus has prepared bread and fishes on
a fire. He invites them for breakfast, even as they struggle
with the catch of 153 big fishes, a number of abundance,
divisible by three (3x51). Jesus gives them the bread and
the fishes and the text says that this was the third time that
Jesus was revealed to the disciples after he was raised from
the dead. This means, the encounter with Mary of Magdala
in the garden is not counted here. Mary, the first witness
of the resurrection, is made completely invisible here.

Then the text goes on to establish Peter in his ministry. Three times Jesus asks Peter "Do you love me?" The first time he asks. "Do you love me more than these?" Three times Peter replies: "Yes Lord, you know that I love you".

The threefold affirmation seems to be necessary to undo the threefold denial in the court of the high priest. Three times he has denied to know Jesus. To the doorkeeper, to the men at the fireplace and to the kinsman of the man whose ear had been cut off. Are you a disciple? "No I am not".

It is this Peter to whom the church is entrusted: Tend my sheep. Mary, running through the streets in search of her beloved, wanting to hold him when she encounters him, has become invisible. Peter's denial has another side which is expressed in what Jesus says in v.18. "Truly, truly, I say to you, when you were young, you girded yourself and walked where you would. But when you are old, you will stretch out your hands and another will gird you and carry you where you do not wish to go". And then he says: "Follow me". The interpreter says that this verse anticipates Peter`s violent death in Rome. It can also mean that the denial of self, of will, of identity, of love, which Peter committed in the court of the high priest, will catch up with him and lead him where he did not intend to go, truly, the footsteps of Jesus.

We know sufficiently well what happened to Peter and his church. We know very little of what happened to Mary from Migdal in Galilee. Some people have proposed that Mary was indeed the disciple whom Jesus loved, whose identity cannot be established in the gospel of John. She, who never denied Jesus, has been denied again and again.

We know today, through feminist scholarship, that this Miryam was a very important leader in the early church. Some popular sources maintain that she traveled as far as today's France, spreading the message of resurrection and uprising. We find it easy to believe in the mission of Thomas who could only believe if he touched. The Kerala church claims to go back to his efforts. We find it difficult to believe in the contribution of Mary who was asked: "Do not hold me, I am going to ascend".

In the nineteenth century, many scriptures were discovered which dated back to the time of the scriptures of the second testament, but had not been included in the canon. Among these scriptures was the Gospel of Mary of Magdala which was found in Egypt. It is incomplete, and we do not clearly know when it was written and by whom. It may have been written in Egypt or in Syria, possibly in the first half of the second century. It has many parallels and similarities with the existing gospels with the difference that it makes the leadership of Mary of Magdala abundantly visible.

There is also one important difference with respect to the concept of mission. In the gospels as we know them, preaching of the kingdom is seen as a way to bring about salvation. In Matthew 24, the disciples are commissioned to preach. Only after this they are warned to guard against error. Finally, they are assured of the coming of the Son of Man. In the Gospel of Mary (8:11-9:4) the order is reversed. First of all, the Saviour cautions the disciples to guard themselves against error. Secondly, he assures them that the seed of true humanity is within them. Only after realising this, they are encouraged to preach.

Mary, who has touched and held earlier, can refrain from touching and let go, but she still believes, hearing her name being called. Realising her humanity must have become extremely difficult in the new situation. Not only did she lose her closest companion, the very fact that she has been pushed into oblivion to such an extent witnesses to her immense loneliness in this church of denying Peters and doubting Thomases. Yet she preached. We know little of what she may have said. But we know what she lived. She stood by her love. She never denied him. She took great risk, being present at the foot of the cross and at the grave. She took risk of ridicule and incredulousness, witnessing to the resurrection. She is still the woman in the garden searching for her loved one, asking us: "Where have you left my Lord"? Where have we left him? Where?

(September 25, 2000)

* * * *

23. TWO PREGNANCIES

Luke 1:26-56

This text builds a bridge between the visit of the angel who announces to Mary that she will fall pregnant and the Song of Mary, which is a song of revolt. This song announces the end of all existing power relationships. Between this visit of the angel and the song of Mary, we find Mary's visit to the hill country to seek support from her elderly cousin Elizabeth. It is the bonding between two very vulnerable women which is of importance here.

Mary at the time of this event must have been very young. She was betrothed to Joseph, but he had not yet taken her home to his own household. She was certainly not expected to be pregnant. She was very scared when the angel greeted her: "Hail Mary, full of Grace. God is with you". He told her that the child she was expecting was going to be a king on the throne of David. She should not be afraid. His name should be Yeshua (God has transcended). He shall be called holy and son of God. The angel also says that Elizabeth, who had been called barren, was pregnant in her sixth month, because "with God nothing is impossible". Mary connects immediately with the vulnerability of her old relative who had been despised for being barren. Elizabeth is now pregnant in a very similar way as Sarah had been pregnant with Isaac (Gen.18:14) or Hannah, the mother of Samuel (I Sam.1:11). While barrenness was a cause of shame, late pregnancy was also in some ways ridiculed, as the very name of Isaac shows. We are dealing here with pregnancies which are offensive to the social order and also outside the realm of what can be expected according to nature.

It is difficult to say what all this means. The catholic church has made a cult of the virgin birth but has had little to say about these unexpected late pregnancies. We know of a more interesting comment on this by the black slave woman Sojourner Truth. She was replying to a clergyman who had objected to equal rights for women on the ground that Jesus was a man. She asked: "Where did your Christ come from? From God and a woman! Man had nothing to do with him!" Indeed, the Bible knows of a number of pregnancies which have nothing to do with a regular family life, they are worked out between a woman and God. Some feminist scholars on the other hand point to a persistent rumour found in Jewish and the Christian ancient literature that Mary was raped by a Roman soldier. None of this can be proved. But we know that Mary has taken an active role in living up to a situation which was fraught with great risk of social ostracism. She says: I am God's servant. Let it be to me according to your word.

Mary goes to her elderly relative in the hill country "with haste". She enters the house of Zechariah and greets Elizabeth. When Elizabeth heard the greeting of Mary, the child leapt in her womb and Elizabeth was filled with the holy spirit and exclaimed loudly: "Blessed are you among women and blessed is the fruit of your womb". She also asks: "Why is it granted to me that the mother of my Lord should come to me? When you greeted me, the child in my womb leapt with joy. Your are blessed because you believed in what God promised to you".

In response to this greeting, Mary replies with the magnificat. She praises God that he has seen the low state of his servant. It is not clear what her lowliness consists of because she is betrothed to Joseph of the house of David and her relative Elizabeth belongs to the daughters of Aaron and Zechariah is a priest. It is likely that her lowliness consists of her youth and an illegitimate pregnancy. She turns this situation into its opposite and says: "Henceforth, all generations will call me blessed, for he who is mighty has done great things for me, and holy is his name. He has scattered the proud in the imagination of their hearts. He has thrown down the mighty from their thrones and made high those who were downcast. He has given dignity to the untouchables. He has filled the hungry with good things and has sent the rich away empty." For Mary, the promise of God becomes visible in a straight line. She remembers the promise of the angel, of which she was very scared. But now Elizabeth's greeting echoes this promise and in a sudden realisation the young girl understands the full significance of what is happening. She realises not only that what the angel told her was true, she also understands that the kingship of which the angel has spoken is totally different from what the kings of Israel stand for. It means the opposite of all the arrogance and violence which goes with power. God literally smashes this power and puts an end to hunger for the poor, while sending the rich away empty. Everything high and low, rich and poor, powerful and powerless is reverted, because God has remembered his compassion and his promise.

This vision of revolt starts from the realisation of these two marginalised women, one young, one old, both vulnerable, that they are at the centre of a new turn of history. The rest of the chapter deals with the birth of John the Baptist and the song of his father Zachariah, who had lost his speech and finds it back to confirm what Elizabeth had already said. The name of the child is <u>Jochanan</u> (John). "God has been merciful, compassionate." He will prepare the way of the Lord and will give salvation to his people in the forgiveness of their sins through the tender mercy of God, - to give light to those who sit in darkness and the shadow of death.

With this vision, the revolt comes to its conclusion: Light is given to those who sit in darkness and in the shadow of death and our feet are guided on the ways of peace. The uprising starts by taking two women out of an undignified situation: The one is young and inexplicably pregnant, the other is old and barren. Each of them is given the strength to bring forth a new life for the salvation of many. With the reversal of their own position, they share a vision of reversal of power relations, not just by putting things upside down, but by creating real peace.

Friday 25th November has been the day to commemorate and fight against the violence against women. Each year around this time massive campaigns are conducted against violence on women. We are so used to this violence that we often believe it is "normal" or "natural", as if nothing can be done about it. The gospel of the first of Advent reminds us that this is not so and that the patriarchal violence is connected with all the violence of class and caste and warfare. Repentance from sins means to do away with this violence, and it is this which ultimately leads our feet on the way to peace. May this peace grow in the imagination of our hearts. Amen.

(November 27, 2005)

24. SOCIAL THIRST AND BEING A SPRING OF LIVING WATER TO OTHERS

John 4: 4-42

Once when Jesus walked through a small town called Samaria, he became thirsty. Physical needs had always been important in the life of Jesus. Hunger, thirst and disease are the cause of much worry for people in life. Jesus too had to fulfill these physical needs. We know that even while hanging on the cross, he said: "I am thirsty."

When Jesus became thirsty in Samaria, it became a social issue. The conflict was about the community. The Jewish community considered the Samaritans as outcastes. No Jew would take anything – not even water- from a Samaritan. If they did so it was considered to be an act of impurity and defilement. Nevertheless, Jesus sat down by a well in Samaria, when his disciples had gone into the town to buy food. A Samaritan woman came to draw water from the well. Jesus asked her: "Will you give me a drink"?

On hearing this, the Samaritan woman was very much surprised. For, if a stranger talked to a woman it would be considered very much shameful. That was the culture of the times. When the disciples of Jesus returned, they were surprised to find him talking to a woman. The Samaritan woman said to Jesus: "You are a Jew and I am a Samaritan woman. How can you ask me for a drink?". Jesus did not give her a clear answer. He told her: "If you knew the gift of God and who it is that asks you for a drink, you would have asked him and he would have given you living water". The woman was perplexed. She could not understand what he meant by living water. As far as she knew, drawing water from the well was a difficult manual labour. She said: "You have nothing to draw with and the well is deep. Where can you get this living water? Are you greater than our father Jacob, who gave us the well?" Jesus answered: "Everyone who drinks this water will be thirsty again, but whoever drinks the water I give him will never thirst. Indeed, the water I give him will become in him a spring of water welling up to eternal life ".

How can we be a spring of water to others? How can we quench their thirst? How can we give strength and courage to others? The divisions and inequalities in the society should no longer be a barrier for us. Even when Jesus had asked for a drink from a Samaritan woman he had cast away her untouchability. Since the person he talked to happened to be a woman, he had cast away her unequal status too. If we could drink the living water offered by Jesus, we would be able to establish solidarity with the oppressed people. The fact is the Samaritan woman could not understand any of these. She was just not interested in doing the difficult job of drawing water. That is why she said to him: "Sir, give me this water so that I won't get thirsty and have to keep coming here to draw water." But Jesus revealed to her that he knew about her life. He told her: "Go, call your husband and come back." "I have no husband", she replied. Jesus knew already that she had had five husbands. He said to her: "You are right when you say you have no husband. The fact is, you have had five husbands, and the man you now have is not your husband. What you have just said is quite true." The woman came to understand that he was a prophet. Immediately her incomplete life got changed into a complete one. She came to feel that neither her religion nor the values with which she was looked at were just. The earlier divisions and differences had become meaningless. She realized she would not consider it hereafter as shameful to be an outcaste or a woman.

The differences like the Samaritan ancestors worshipping the Lord at the mountain and the Jews worshipping him in Jerusalem, were of no importance to her thereafter. Jesus told her, "Believe me, woman, a time is coming when you will worship the Father neither on this mountain nor in Jerusalem. The true worshippers will worship the Father in spirit and truth...". The Samaritan woman said, "I know that the Messiah (called Christ) is coming. When he comes, he will explain everything to us." Then Jesus revealed his identity to her: "I who speak to you am he."

How could we, who have heard this story, follow Jesus? How could we live here after?

1. There should be no inequality among us. We should do what we can to bring about an equitable society.

2. Women should not remain oppressed within our midst. Women studying theology, should have the right to get ordained if they so desire. Christian women have to be part of women's struggles in the secular world and must join national women's rights movements.

3. There must be equal rights for Dalits within the Christian church. Dalits still do not have sufficient representation in decision making within the church.

4. If we yearn to follow Christ, we should give up our interest in religious expansionism. We cannot be communalists.

We certainly need the help of the Holy Spirit to attain all these four objectives. However, we ought to have faith and desire for the spirit.

* * * *

V. BEYOND STRUCTURAL SIN

25. TEMPTATIONS OF POWER AND WEAKNESS

Luke 22:24-46

The text of Luke 22:24-46 speaks of a situation in which the State is prepared to come down on the Jesus movement. Jesus and the disciples are facing a qualitative change in their lives. While they have been able to move and work with a certain amount of freedom so far, they now enter directly into a situation of persecution. The last supper itself is a sign of this situation of transition from sharing in the community of the meal to sharing in the community of suffering and persecution. The text speaks partly about the conversations which are going on around the last supper and partly it leads us into the events which directly precede the arrest of Jesus.

To start with there are two types of temptations which go with this situation: The one is not to understand the seriousness of the problems faced and to indulge in internal power struggles. The other temptation is to understand the seriousness but to cave in under it by betrayal, by resort to violence or by slipping into despair and inaction.

As the temptations listed here are of a characteristic nature, it will be useful to go through them one by one. The first temptation (v.24:27) is the competition about ranking. Who is the greatest? Jesus compares this attitude to the kings of the Gentiles: "The kings of the gentiles exercise lordship over them and those in authority over them are called benefactors". This is a common temptation

in the church as well: to exert authority and to be called
benefactors. Jesus counterposes this attitude with his own
values to serve at the table.   Actually, this is a feminist
image. The women who serve at the table are never seen
in a position of authority. They are not even perceived as
doing good to others. Jesus thus tells of a service which
goes unnoticed and which neither is based on power nor
gives control over people.

Jesus acknowledges that the disciples have stood by
him in his trials. Throughout his work, there has been the
expectation on him to use his power, to turn bread into
stones. If this is refused, then disappointment and mistrust
have to be dealt with. God's kingdom and the community
of the meal belong to those who do not use their power in
this way.

However, for those who do not use their power, another
temptation is in store: the temptation to be overwhelmed
by weakness. Jesus compares this to the image of being
sifted like wheat. He says to Simon: "I have prayed for
you that your faith may not fail and when you have turned
again, strengthen your brethren". The very formulation of
Jesus' prayer for Simon expresses his knowledge that Simon
will deny him before the cock crows. However, he also
knows that this weakness will not be the last word. Simon
will turn round and strengthen his brethren.

The third type of temptation of which the text speaks
has to with the problem of how to face one's own weakness
internally, and how to face the external threat. As a first
step, Jesus tells the disciples to be on their guard. If he had
told them earlier to go without bag, purse or sandals, he
now tells them to be prepared to buy a sword. He knows

that he and his disciples will be reckoned among the transgressors. He knows that people's support will not be forthcoming.

However, this text is not about armed resistance. When the disciples later use the sword to prevent his arrest, he stops them from using it and heals the ear of the sentry which has been severed. The significant advice of Jesus is: "Pray that you may not enter into temptation". He says this two times, but his advice goes unheeded. Jesus tries to fortify his disciples against both the temptations mentioned above. Neither does he want them to be overwhelmed with fear nor does he want them to rely on the use of force. However, the disciples are unable to face the situation. They sleep off in weariness. It is only Jesus himself who stays awake to face his weakness. He finds the disciples asleep in their sorrow. It is due to this despondence and unpreparedness that they try to resist Jesus' captors with arms. But he stops them and heals the wounded man instead.

What do we learn from this text in today's situation? The economic policies have so much turned against people that "doing good" to people is no longer easy. The state is turning against the common people and it is not longer possible to act as middlemen and go-between and to be seen as benefactors. Whoever tries to work towards the table fellowship of God's kingdom, whoever talks of the rights of the common people, can be seen as traitor and transgressor. It is a time in which trade union leaders are murdered and unions fighting for people's rights are persecuted for anti-state activities. In this situation, we may face the other two temptations which Jesus expresses.

We may be tempted to back out and cave in because the situation is so overwhelmingly against us. Even if this should happen to us, Jesus tells us, like Peter, that we can turn again and strengthen our people. We may also be tempted to turn violent, but there is no solution in this.

We are also told that we have to be alert, that resistance may be heavy. The times in which talking about social justice was well received, may have come to an end. We may have to be prepared to face hostility. At the same time we are told that we cannot rely on force. We have to learn that AK 47s cannot solve the problem of social justice. But we are also not allowed to give way to our weariness, to sleep off in our anxiety. Probably this is the most tiresome part that we have to be awake and prepared to act all the time. Let us try to listen to the words of Jesus: "Why do you sleep? Rise and pray that you may not enter into temptation". Amen.

(November 6, 1991)

* * * *

26. UNRIGHTEOUS MAMMON AND TRUE RICHES

Luke 16: 1-13

The theme of the passage is found in verse 13: "You cannot serve God and Mammon." This is an archaic expression. The right equivalent for the Greek word that refers to worldly wealth is "Capital" or "Investment." So, the correct wording should have been: "You cannot serve both God and capital." Though we find a similar passage in the gospel of Matthew, I would like to base my study on the passage in Luke, since Luke generally stands up against the rich and speaks up for the poor, joining hands with them.

"You cannot serve both God and money ", is the most significant part of the whole parable. Moreover, it happens to be an introduction to the parable of the poor Lazarus. The chapter's message is that whoever follows the laws of capital and profit is separated from God.

Once I had the occasion to witness a play depicting the situation of a village. There was a money lender in the play, whose assistant forged the loan documents of the poor people. While the poor in fact got only small sums of money as loans, the assistant made entries of big amounts against their names in the documents executed. If he gave someone a sum of fifty rupees, the entry made was one hundred rupees. He used to appropriate the extra interest amount accruing out of it. The very next day of witnessing the play, we had the occasion to read this passage from the Bible. We were reminded of the scene in the play and it made us laugh. While the man in the play had collected money, the man in the parable redeemed people from debts.

Since the servant of God (mentioned in the Bible) spent money irresponsibly, people called him "unjust." However, in verse 8 Jesus lauds him and says he had acted shrewdly. The "master" referred to here is "kyrios" according to the original language manuscript. The interpreters of the Bible are of the opinion that it could be translated as "Jesus". While it is surprising that Jesus praised a servant called unjust by others, there is a great truth in what he said. Jesus calls "unjust" the capital and the profit derived out of it. What he means is that while capital is unjust, it is possible to gain friends through it if it is used without any profit motive. He proposes compassion and generosity. In verse 9 Jesus says: "I tell you, use worldly wealth to gain friends for yourselves, so that when it is gone, you will be welcomed into eternal dwellings."

Let us look at verses 10 to 12 on the basis of verse 13: "Nobody can serve both God and money. Either he will hate the one and love the other.... "This is not found in the original manuscript. But Luke summarizes the whole thing succinctly at the end: "Whoever can be trusted with very little can also be trusted with much..." Many a time verse 10 is used as a separate proverb without considering it as part of the parable. Then, what should one be faithful to, according to Jesus? Should we serve God or capital? Should one earn a profit on each and every paisa or should one be trusting in God? When we use money without any profit motive, we must act with a sense of accommodating the interests of others. That is the meaning of being faithful to God.

In verse 11, the question is raised again: "So if you have not been faithful to God in handling the unrighteous mammon, who will entrust you with true riches?" It is not possible to be faithful to God and at the same time to have a profit motive. Verse 12 stresses it again: "And if you have not been trustworthy with someone else's property, who will give you property of your own"? This has to be seen in a class perspective. God wants us to be answerable to those who are vulnerable and are crushed by exploitation. That is, if we are not faithful to God in handling the money of others handed over to us, how are we going to attain real life or the Kingdom of God. This is clearly the opposite of accumulating money by *Kanduvatti* (extortion by daily interest payment) or any other way of squeezing the poor.

I remember what Bishop Selvamony once told us: "It is a big flaw that we do not have a theological thinking on matters like accounting. For all of us are pushed into the management of the church. Therefore, the 16th chapter of Luke could be taken as the basis for management theology."

The biblical passage does not say: "Do not handle money." On the contrary, it only says: "Handle it differently." Create a society that has no profit motive and exploitation. It is impossible to serve God and capital at the same time. We have to learn how to use the money against the capitalist system. For that we have to learn how to be faithful to God. It is difficult, but it is the right thing to do.

* * * *

27. FREEDOM FROM FEAR

Psalms 86

This Psalm sounds very much like a psalm of personal prayer and meditation. It is popular for personal prayer because it seems to have all the crucial elements: personal relationship with God, praise of God, and protection from evil. It seems to be a psalm which gives us security and peace of mind. However, if we go deeper, I believe it is a psalm which in fact disturbs our security and peace of mind. It is a psalm which can stir us up to question all our values. The psalm starts by saying: (v 1) "Answer me, for I am poor and needy". What are we to make of this? The psalms were not written by the poor and powerless. Does this mean that it speaks about spiritual poverty?

No, the palmist has to say I am poor and needy in order to be heard by God, because God indeed, is on the side of the poor and needy. This is shown by the history of the exodus and the prophets. So in order to be heard by God we must identify with the poor and needy. So our first problem if we pray this psalm is: can we expect to be heard by God? Are we on the side of the poor and needy? Our solidarity with the poor and needy is a crucial part of our personal relationship with God. The personal is political. The next question is raised by the praise of God. Often our praise of God is a matter of routine. God does wondrous things, what does it mean anyway. But the praise here is on the promise of change of society. All nations will come and bow down before God.   All nations will finally bow down before the God who is on the side of the poor. This means society has to change very radically, a new International Economic order is necessary, our own society of profit and exploitation has to be rebuilt. So the disturbing question arises: Do we really believe that change in possible, do we believe in God's wonders! Often we say: Anyway, everything is sinful, nothing changes. But only if we believe that change is possible, can we praise God`s name.

The next and most crucial disturbance comes from v.11: "Teach me thy way O Lord that I walk in thy truth. Unite my heart that I fear thy name". God's ways are not our ways, God's faith is often very different from what we make of it. The Psalmist prays: "Unite my heart that I fear Thy name". What does this mean? It means first of all that we should be single-minded about God`s will.  There are so many distractions and compulsions.  Often we are just opportunistic.  Often there is the temptation to do things for money. But the need is to be single-minded, to have the point of orientation of God`s will. But what does it mean here to fear God`s name? Does it mean that we do things out of fear of punishment? Fearing the name means, on the contrary to be free from all fear because the name means: I shall be with you. If we are free from fear because God is with us, then we can afford to be open minded.

If we start a new semester we need to pray for openness. Let us be open to what we study, let us be open to listen to one another. It is necessary not to be frightened of scientific ways of reading the bible. Let us not be frightened of politics, let us not be frightened to search for new ways, let us not be frightened of authority.

This prayer for openness is also necessary when it comes to the question of "enemies", which is mentioned in the final verses. The church is ridden by strife and enmity, petty quarrels and court cases. Even in a seminary there is gossip, scheming, fear to lose face. I think the sign of favor for which we can ask from God is freedom from fear. Let us not be frightened to face conflict if we side with the poor. Let us not be frightened to take risks. Let us feel free to believe that change is possible. Let us feel free to obey God more than human beings. Let us be free from fear of the rules of the institutions, of examiners and mark sheets. If we become free from fear our personal prayer will reach out to others, we will be able to change ourselves and our environment. May God give us an open mind.

Amen.

* * * *

28. THE CITY OF THE POOR

Psalm 34

This Psalm is ascribed to David when he was pretending to be mad in front of Achish of Gath (not Abimelech) as it is reported in 1 Sam.21:12-15. David is fleeing from Saul and the priest Abimelech gives him holy bread and the sword with which earlier David had defeated Goliath. But when David comes to Achish, the king of Gath, the servants of the king recognise and report him and David is much afraid of Achish. So much so, that he feigns madness and the king sends him away. The priest Abimelech who has helped David to escape from Saul, is later slain by the Edomite Doeg on the command of Saul together with 84 other priests of the city of Nod. In fact Doeg razes the whole city to the ground. Thus, the heading of the psalm refers to a situation of utmost persecution and fear of death. However, it is likely that the psalm was written as a literary poem because the verses follow alphabetic order.

The psalm starts with the praise of God. "I will bless the Lord all my life. His praise shall continuously be in my mouth". It goes immediately further and addresses itself to the afflicted, the anavim, as it is called in Hebrew. Some of us still remember that Fr. Kappen the liberation theologian from Kerala, was editing a journal under this title - Anavim the afflicted. The singer calls the anavim "O magnify the Lord with me, and let us exalt his name together" (v.3).

The reason is given in a very personal way: I sought the Lord and he answered me and delivered me from all my fears. Freedom from fear, Al tirah, fear not, - this is the main appeal of this psalm. Look at him and be radiant, so your faces shall never be ashamed (v.5). When God leads the children of Israel out of slavery, he goes ahead of them in a column of fire. He reveals himself in Sinai in the burning bush. No one can see God face to face. But if we look to him, a reflection of his radiance will be on us. The very name of God is: I shall be with you. If God is with us, our face will not fall, we will not be ashamed.

The singer says of himself: This poor man cried and the Lord heard him and saved him out of all his troubles (v.6). V.7 elaborates on this process of salvation: The angel of the Lord encamps around those who fear him and delivers them. The image which is used here is the tent, the camp during the exodus, the camp in warfare. A wall of solidarity. Not the fortress of psalm 46 but a tent wall, something very temporary and mobile. The deliverance will be with those who fear God. Al tirah, fear not. The Lord has delivered me of all my fears. Those who fear God are truly free from fear.

While we associate fear usually with terror and trembling, the deeper meaning is most comprehensively summed up in Deut.10:12 and 13. "And now Israel what does the Lord your God require of you, but to fear the Lord your God, to walk in all his ways, to love him, to serve the Lord your God with all your heart and with all your soul". Thus, the explanation implies to walk in his ways to love, to serve with heart and soul, i.e. with every heartbeat and with every breath. This concentration on

God's ways itself helps to be in touch with his messages and to be surrounded by his wings. God's goodness can be tasted, his refuge gives a sense of release.

Those who fear God - love God, serve God, walk in his ways- suffer no want. Though they are migrants through the desert or refugees like David, they suffer no want. V.10 works out the contrast - the young lions suffer want and hunger. The predators, those who pray on others - another version of the text says "the rich" - and it is quite possible that the young lions are an image for the rich - they want more and more, meat, consumer goods, amusements, thrills. But those who seek the Lord lack no good thing.

In v.11-14 the singer works out the pedagogy of the fear of the Lord. First of all it is made clear that the fear of the Lord is not a life insurance. Neither can we hope for a long life, nor can we hope to enjoy good. This is not part of the bargain. This sounds like a direct contradiction to v.8 where goodness and happiness can be tasted. The emphasis here is not on our emotions but on what we *do*.

V.13-14, Keep your tongue from evil and your lips from speaking deceit. Depart from evil and do good. Seek peace, and pursue it. It is not as if such endeavour will immediately be rewarded with success. The only assurance is that God will *see* and *hear*.

V.15-22 counterposes the righteous and the evil doer. The evil doer will be forgotten, his remembrance will be cut from the earth. The righteous will be heard and delivered.

However, this deliverance goes through tremendous crisis, v.18. The Lord is near to the broken-hearted. He saves the crushed in spirit. With this reference to the broken-hearted and the crushed in spirit we are back to the afflicted, to the *anavim* who are addressed in the beginning of the psalm and are exhorted to join in the praise   God.

V.19 emphasizes the difficulties even more. Many are the afflictions of the righteous, the zaddik who walks in the ways of God. But the Lord delivers him out of all those afflictions. He keeps all his bones, none of them shall be broken.

At the same time, evil shall slay the wicked. The text does not say that God shall slay the wicked or that the righteous shall be redeemed. The root *padah* which is used here, does not mean salvation from sin but redemption from slavery.

This psalm is in a peculiar way connected to the life and death of Jesus. Jesus, obviously, has been a zaddik, a just man, who feared and loved the Lord, walked in his ways and served him. But has the angel of the Lord encamped around him? Not, obviously, in the way as Satan envisaged it in the story of the temptation: Throw yourself down from this wall and the angels of God will serve you.

Psalm 34:20 is quoted in John 19:36. It refers to the death on the cross before the Sabbath starts. The other two men who died with him had their legs broken to hasten their death. But Jesus was already dead, so his legs remained intact. But one of the soldiers pierced his side with a spear and blood and water came out (v.34). Is there any meaning in this protection of all the bones even if the person is dead? The only meaning I can see is that even in death the wholeness and integrity of the dead person has to be faced. See this man. He is not a mass of dead flesh. This refers to another quote from Zachariah 12.

V.10 (... when they look on the one whom they have pierced, they shall mourn for him...). The overall context of this quote is described in Zach.12:10-13. The chapter deals with salvation of Jerusalem which is under siege. But on that day which Zachariah promises, a shield will be put around the inhabitants of Jerusalem so that the feeble will be strong like David, the house of David like God and like the angel of the Lord. However, this is only possible if a very drastic change comes over Jerusalem herself.

The spirit of compassion and supplication shall come upon Jerusalem. They will look at him whom they have pierced, they shall mourn for him as one mourns for an only child and weep bitterly over him as one weeps over a first-born. It is not clear to whom this refers. Who is this suffering servant over whom they weep, we do not know. But it will be such a big mourning as the mourning for Hadad-rimmon in the plain of Megiddo. This refers to a big festival of the Canaanites which deals with the death and resurrection of the God Hadad. Everybody in Jerusalem has to participate in the mourning. This mourning will be for the suffering of the zaddik, the just. Psalm 34 says clearly that the just will be severely afflicted The affliction may be leading to death. But redemption is possible if the whole society faces the injustice which is being done and is capable of mourning. In most societies the task of mourning has been left to the women. The men tear their clothes or put ashes on their forehead but the women will cry and wail. In our society, the Dalit men have gone to announce the death, they also dance in front of the house of mourning, the women wail. Thus, it is the women and the Dalits who have been singled out to face the pain of death and mourning. But in the vision of Zachariah all will mourn, each house in Israel, separately and women and men separately. Each section will have to face the pain of death and mourning on their own. Nobody else will do it for them.

Only if society as a whole faces the injustice it inflicts on the righteous, redemption can take place. This brings us back to the beginning. We started with David who had to flee from Saul. The whole city of Nod was put to the sword because they helped David.

David was not an ideal king but he could repent and correct himself. He was himself an afflicted man who could call on the afflicted: Magnify the Lord with me and let us exalt his name together.

Amen.

(July 18, 1996)

* * * *

29. ABRAM BLESSED, SARAI BETRAYED AND RESCUED

Genesis 12

1. The Background

Gen. 12 is the chapter which forms a bridge between the story of the origins of humankind and the story of the fathers which leads into the history of Israel. This covenant is based on God's promise never again to curse the ground or destroy all living creatures (Gen. 8:21b-22). However, even this promise of the covenant with Noah is later undermined by the attempt to build cities and a tower to touch the sky. Upon this, the confusion of languages occurs and the people are scattered all over the earth (Gen.11:1-9). This is the background for the geneaology of Abram which forms the end of Gen.11 (v.27-32).

Normally this chapter is read as an admonition for steadfastness in faith. However, the arch father betrays the promise of God. We can therefore propose to read this chapter as a parody on the cultural values of men protecting women, women being made sex objects and being valued for their fertility. God runs down all these cultural values by making them into a practical joke.

2. The Blessing on Abram

Gen.12 sets in with the call to Abram: "Go away from your country and your father's house to the land that I will show you, and I will make you a great nation, and I will bless you, and make your name great, so that you will be a blessing. I will bless those who bless you, and him who curse you, he who curses you, and by you all the families of the earth shall bless themselves". This is a very comprehensive blessing. On the other hand it is made clear that this does not mean the power to subjugate other nations, on the contrary: I will make your name great *so that you will be a blessing.*

God promises: "I will bless those who bless you and him who curses you, I will curse". This promise, as we will see later, Abram himself does not seem to remember when he is visited by crisis. "By you all families of the earth shall bless themselves". This widens the blessing to the horizon of humanity as a whole, beyond the "nation" which Abram is supposed to become.

Verses 4-9 narrate the migrations of Abram, Sarai and Lot, from Haran to Canaan. They came to Shechem, to a sacred tree at Moreh and God promises to Abram that he will give this land to his descendents (v.7). East of Bethel and West of Ai, Abram builds an altar as a symbol of this promise and then travels on towards the Negev.

3. Sarai Betrayed

The next incisive event is narrated in v.10-16. A famine strikes the land, and Abram decides to move on to Egypt in order to escape starvation. At this point, a very incisive break occurs in the relationship between Abram and Sarai. We hear that Sarai is a woman very beautiful to behold. So while entering Egypt, Abram indoctrinates his wife to lie about their relationship. He says: "You are beautiful. When the Egyptians see you as my wife, they will kill me. Say you are my sister, so it may go well with me because of you and that my life will be spared on your account" (v.12 & 13).

Abram makes an appeal to save his skin, but he does it at the cost of her physical integrity. It is clear that she will be sexually used by the Egyptians. His betrayal is twofold: He is willing to hand her over to the Egyptians in order to be treated well himself. He also forgets the part of the blessing which says: "I will bless those who bless you and him who curses you, I will curse". And so it happens. The Egyptians see that Sarai is very beautiful, the princes of Pharoah's praise her to Pharoah, she ends up in Pharoah's harem, while her "brother" is compensated with sheep, oxen, asses and servants and has a good time.

4. The Parallels: The Mother Betrayed

This part of the narrative, where the "Mother" of Israel is in jeopardy, has two parallels. The same motive comes again in Gen.20 and 26. In Gen.20 we are told that Abraham and Sarah are journeying towards the Negev and Abraham says of his wife that she is his sister, whereupon King Abimelech of Gerar took Sarah. In this chapter, Abimelech is warned in a dream that Sarah is Abraham's wife and that he will perish if he touches her. Because of this, he restores her to Abraham and sends husband and wife away with sheep, oxen and slaves and a thousand pieces of silver. In Gen.26, we hear another version of this story where Isaac goes to Gerar and pretends that his wife Rebekah is his sister. However, Isaac is observed fondling his wife and the king calls the bluff. In each of these narratives, the king asks the husband in consternation: "What is it that you have done to me? Why did you not tell me that she was your wife?"

5. Sarai Restored

The version in Gen.12 is the most drastic one. Here it is
suggested that Sarai has been sexually used. In this chapter
we hear that after this violation, God afflicts Pharoah with
plagues because of Sarai, Abram's wife. The use of
language here is similar as in the story of the Exodus, where
the house of Pharoah is slain with plagues to "Let my
people go". Here, Pharoah's house is slain with plague,
"to let the mother go". At the same time, the Pharoah in
Gen.12, as King Abimelech in chapter 20 and 26, is shown
in a rather helpless position asking, "What is it that you
have done to me?" It is as if Pharoah is under the spell of
God's promise to Abraham: "I will bless those who bless
you and him who curses you, I will curse". God keeps the
promise which Abram has failed to remember in times of
crisis. It is Abram, the Father of Israel and of humanity,
honoured by Jews, Christians and Muslims, who cuts the
poorest figure in this picture. The chapter which starts
with a most comprehensive blessing, ends in
embarrassment. The culturally expected role of the husband
"protecting" his wife is reverted. The husband benefits from
the beauty of his wife by telling a lie and requesting her to
lie. At the same time, the narrator sees to it that the integrity
of the mother is vindicated and restored by God's
intervention. The abysses of patriarchy opening up in this
chapter are heart rending. God's promise has to grow wings
to traverse the abyss.

6. God's promise is finally fulfilled in the covenant with
Abraham and Sarah (Gen.Ch.17), where their names are
also changed from Abram and Sarai to Abraham and Sarah.
This covenant comes after the sad narrative in which Hagar,

the slave woman, is used as a substitute womb and then driven away (Ch.16). This chapter of Hagar shows yet again how even Sarah is enslaved to the pressure of having to provide a heir. As she cannot overcome her barrenness, she abuses her slave woman and then drives her away out of shame. The continuous promise of their own biological child for Abraham and Sarah appears as a joke, when God says that he will bless Sarah with a child. Abraham falls on his face and laughs because both were beyond the age of child bearing (Ch.17:17). Likewise, Sarah, when the angels visit their tent at Mamre, laughs at the promise of a child (18:12).

The blessing in the beginning of ch.12 only gets fulfilled after physical beauty and fertility have been worn out. God's blessing appears as a practical joke undermining the patriarchal values of virility combined with woman as a sex object and child bearing machine. We are still struggling to live down these values.

May God Bless us with his sense of humour. Amen.

(August 22, 2002)

* * * *

30. THE CHRIST PSALM RE-READ THROUGH TAMAR'S EYES

Philippians 2:1-11, Genesis 38

1. Introduction

According to the order of the CSI, we are today celebrating Jesus' capacity to bring about peace and justice. This is a tall order while the bombardments in Afghanistan are in full swing. Our own country is war-torn not only in Kashmir but also by partition-like conflagrations in Malegaon (Nasik Dt. Maharashtra). Apart from this, we also commemorate this week Reformation Day, remembering the need to question our faith and renew it. For the Methodist churches as well as the Syrians, it is Family Sunday. This reminds us that the questions of war and peace are not only raging at international levels, but justice and peace often elude us at the family level as well. Violence can be rampant in most intimate relationships.

The main text prescribed for this Sunday is Phil.2:1-11. This is certainly a challenge to reflect on war, peace and justice. At the same time it is a text about which feminists have raised questions. We need to read it in a new perspective. This is why I have complemented it with the story of Tamar in Gen.38. I have to admit that it is unusual to deal with this second text on Family Sunday. But perhaps this, then, is the Reformation content of our reflection. Renewing our faith in the light of something unexpected.

2. The Christ Psalm

The initial verses of Phil.2 are admonishing the congregation to be in one spirit. The congregation in Philippi was not poor, it consisted of people who were relatively well off and who financially supported Paul. He is writing to them from jail. We do not know for sure where he was imprisoned while he wrote this letter, but it is quite likely that it could have been in Ephesus. The main thought of this particular passage is that he wants the congregation to overcome their divisiveness and to unite in the spirit of Christ, which is then exemplified in this Psalm consisting of the verses 6-11 which are probably not written by Paul but which was already available to him. This Psalm is a key text in Christian preaching about humility and it is therefore useful to remember that it was not written to a congregation which was poor or which had a harbour proletariate like the congregation in Corinth. It was written to a well-off new congregation without much experience. There could have been competition among the new members to excel in the new faith, perhaps a certain over enthusiasm of a new beginning. One of the key topics in this letter is joy and rejoicing despite the jail background. Apart from this there is also the warning of the false teachings.

I would like to connect the contents of this Psalm with what my guru Dr.M.M.Thomas, again and again was preaching to the churches - inclined towards self-righteousness and triumphalism - about Isaiah 53 and its connection with the life or Jesus. M.M. never tired to point out that Jesus was not the conquering king, he chose to be the suffering servant. It is this path which Paul wants the congregation in Philippi to follow: To refrain from self righteousness, to learn humility, to listen to others. But is this what is happening in the church, in society? Are we not constantly involved in a struggle for the survival of the fittest? Most of the time humility is being preached to those who are already powerless anyway. We are preaching humility to women, to Dalits, to Adivasis, to workers in the unorganised sector, to people of other faiths. This is what feminist theologians have objected to. Teaching humility to the humiliated does not add up to liberation. At the same time, the arrogance of the powerful goes on. Sometimes, the self-righteous style themselves as suffering servants. The ambiguity is enormous.

This is happening even at the world level right now. The United States is the most powerful nation in the world, economically, politically and in terms of armed might. But their rulers perceive themselves as victims and saviours simultaneously. While it is understandable that people are under shock after the attacks of September 11th 2001, it is still astonishing how short the historical memory is. We remember another September 11th way back in 1973, when La Moneda, the Presidential palace of Santiago de Chile, was bombed in order to dislodge the democratically elected regime of President Salvador Allende and to install the fascist dictator General Augusto Pinochet in power, whose reign of terror lasted for one and a half decades. The country was littered with the broken lives of tens of thousands of people tortured, murdered and disappeared. All this happened on instigation of the nation which is now "defending its lifestyle" and "democracy" with high sounding campaigns of "infinite justice" and "enduring freedom". Historical memory has also forgotten that the Taliban were a creation of the US against the Russian backed Najibulla regime, a regime liquidated with even greater brutality than the Allende government. Now both sides are pitted against each other in a spiral of violence, each fighting a "Holy War", each ready for a fight to the finish.

In the light of this deadlock everybody needs to introspect and question their own values. "When they hit you, hit back" may no longer work in this situation. Some fundamental doubts have to be raised about the logic of violence itself. We remember Mahatma Gandhi's saying: "An eye for an eye leaves everybody blind." This is certainly true. But can non-violence deliver the goods? Is it viable? How can it be practiced? The movements who have resisted the war in the US have campaigned with the slogan: "Violence is a failure of imagination". How then can we spurn our imagination for non-violent disobedience? It is at this point that I would like to draw on the story of Tamar in Gen.38.

3. The Story of Tamar

Tamar's story comes as a separate episode inserted into the narrative of Jacob and Esau towards the end. More specifically, it deals with Judah, one of the sons of Jacob who was instrumental in selling his brother Joseph to the Israelites who then took Joseph to Egypt and sold him. In the meantime, their father Jacob is desperate thinking that his son has been killed, as the brothers have shown him the bloodstained garment of Joseph.

It is at this point that Tamar comes in. The story of Tamar starts with a genealogy. We hear that Judah had married a Cannanite woman and had three sons with her whom she names Er, Onam and Shela. Judah gives Er, a wife called Tamar. We hear (v.7) that Er was wicked in the

eyes of the Lord and that the Lord slew him. This is an
important remark as normally a widow will be blamed for
her husband's untimely death. According to the custom of
the Levirate, a childless young widow had to be given to
the younger brother of the deceased husband in order to
safeguard the lineage. But Onam did not want to create
offspring for his brother, he only used Tamar`s body and
spilled his seed. He too, we are told, was slain by the
Lord. Now Judah gets scared for his third son and sends
Tamar to her parents' house as a widow. This is against
the Hebrew law. He promises to give his third son as a
husband later, but he does not mean it.

In the meantime, Judah's wife also dies and he is
widowed. In many languages, like in Tamil, there is only
a word for "widow". This indicates a woman which is
seen as inauspicious, to be kept under social controls. There
is no word for "widower". Men whose wives die are easily
remarried. Judah finishes his period of mourning and goes
to his sheep shearers in Timnah. When Tamar hears of
this, she dresses up as a prostitute and sits at the road to
Timnah, because she knows that though Shela has grown
up, Judah will not give him to her so that she can have
children. Judah, seeing her, thinks she is a harlot and
negotiates a price for using her body. He will send her a
kid from the flock, he says. In the meantime, Tamar asks
for a pledge to be given to her till he sends the kid. So he
gives his signet, his cord and his staff as a pledge. He has
intercourse, she gets pregnant and returns to her parents
house, putting on the clothes of her widowhood. When
Judah sends the kid as promised through his friend, the
harlot cannot be found. People say there is no such woman
in this area. They give up on search in order to avoid

ridicule. Some time later news reaches Judah that his daughter in law Tamar is pregnant. He is furious, prepared to pull her out of the house and to have her burned. However, when she faces him, she presents to him his signet, his cord and his staff and says: "He to him this belongs, is the father of my child". Seeing this evidence he acknowledges her right: "She is more just than me". The end of the chapter tells that Tamar gives birth to twins. Thus, her childlessness is thoroughly overcome. What is striking is that Tamar takes her life into her own hands and gets what is her due. While doing this she shows utmost courage, but no vengefulness. She cheats as she has been cheated but she does no harm. In the end she stands justified in the eyes of the community who was prepared to kill her.

4. I would like to read these two texts in each other's light. Let us look at the Christ psalm of Phil. 2:5-11 in the light of Tamar's story. One thing which strikes me is that Tamar takes her own initiative. She brings the culprit to book and gets her due. She does not remain a victim. In the Christ Psalm, we have the self denial and the obedience which lead to death. The initiative is then entirely with God. God intervenes and raises the Christ, makes his name higher than all other names, so that in his name all knees shall bend. This intervention also creates a new problem of the Lordship of Christ the King, promoted by the Church, under which the suffering servant is in danger of becoming invisible. If we look at the Christ Psalm in the light of Tamar's story we also notice one important difference: Tamar herself brings the culprit to book and makes him answerable. In the passion narrative of Jesus, he remains the victim. The culprits go scot free, they are not made

answerable. This raises the question: Where is justice? Peace and justice can be affirmed in the light of the resurrection, but they remain elusive in the here and now. When Jesus says about his tormentors: "Father forgive, they know not what they are doing", he expresses forgiveness. But where is peace, where is reconciliation, where is justice?

After the end of apartheid in South Africa, a Truth Commission was instituted to give the victims a voice and to make restitution and amnesty possible so that the cycle of violence could be broken. This was an extremely painful and deficient process, but it saved society from some of the madness of pain, anger and revenge which might otherwise have led to the breakdown of civil society. It made introspection possible and to some extent, healing.

Tamar has the bold imagination to take her right without violating anybody else's right. She cheats by concealing her identity but there is no falsehood in her. Looking at her in the light of the Christ-psalm the question arises: Is she ruthless, does she take her right as a thing to be grasped? Clearly, the answer is no, because she only risks her own life, not anybody else's. Her faith is such that she has the courage to stake her life, her honour, he very existence in society. She does this in order to create life for herself and for future generations. It is by this bold act that she makes her way into the genealogy of Jesus in Matt.1, becoming the fore-mother of the Christ whose praise is sung in Phil.2. May she inspire us to have the courage to take risks for peace and justice non-violently. May she inspire our power of imagination to create new life in the midst of strife and war.   Amen.

(October 28, 2001)

www.ingramcontent.com/pod-product-compliance
Lightning Source LLC
Chambersburg PA
CBHW022131080426
42734CB00006B/311